The struggle not just to define but also to preserve American power is no modern phenomenon: questions of intervention and projection have dominated the nation's politics from the days of the Founding Fathers. Then, as now, the old centres of power were shifting. Nor is economic stress an unfamiliar factor for policymakers. As another presidential election looms, America's role in global affairs and security has emerged as one of the campaign's great battle lines.

But in 2012, domestic political and economic problems are compounded by the ongoing financial crisis in Europe, which, together with the overstretch and fatigue from two wars, has sapped the strength of America's chief allies. While it may urge its NATO partners to shoulder more of the security burden, the US finds them less willing and occasionally unable to share the strain. This *Adelphi* examines the myriad challenges America must confront if it is to uphold and spread its values and interests.

D0366589

Weary policeman: American power in an age of austerity

Dana H. Allin and Erik Jones

Weary policeman: American power in an age of austerity

Dana H. Allin and Erik Jones

IISS The International Institute for Strategic Studies

The International Institute for Strategic Studies

Arundel House | 13–15 Arundel Street | Temple Place | London | WC2R 3DX | UK

First published July 2012 by **Routledge**
4 Park Square, Milton Park, Abingdon, Oxon, OX14 4RN

for **The International Institute for Strategic Studies**
Arundel House, 13–15 Arundel Street, Temple Place, London, WC2R 3DX, UK
www.iiss.org

Simultaneously published in the USA and Canada by **Routledge**
270 Madison Ave., New York, NY 10016

Routledge is an imprint of Taylor & Francis, an Informa Business

© 2012 The International Institute for Strategic Studies

DIRECTOR-GENERAL AND CHIEF EXECUTIVE Dr John Chipman
EDITOR Dr Nicholas Redman
ASSISTANT EDITOR Janis Lee
EDITORIAL Dr Jeffrey Mazo, Carolyn West, Sarah Johnstone, Dr Ayse Abdullah
COVER/PRODUCTION John Buck
COVER IMAGES iStockphoto: Randall Allen, EdStock2, Kirby Hamilton, manley099, maogg, Kivilcim Pinar, PeskyMonkey, Adam Smigielski; Dreamstime: Gary Blakeley, Kentannenbaum, Karin Hildebrand Lau, Misty Pfeil; Liu Jin/AFP/Getty Images; J. Scott Applewhite/AP/Press Association Images; US Navy/Eric Powell.

The International Institute for Strategic Studies is an independent centre for research, information and debate on the problems of conflict, however caused, that have, or potentially have, an important military content. The Council and Staff of the Institute are international and its membership is drawn from almost 100 countries. The Institute is independent and it alone decides what activities to conduct. It owes no allegiance to any government, any group of governments or any political or other organisation. The IISS stresses rigorous research with a forward-looking policy orientation and places particular emphasis on bringing new perspectives to the strategic debate.

The Institute's publications are designed to meet the needs of a wider audience than its own membership and are available on subscription, by mail order and in good book-shops. Further details at www.iiss.org.

Printed and bound in Great Britain by Bell & Bain Ltd, Thornliebank, Glasgow

All rights reserved. No part of this book may be reprinted or reproduced or utilised in any form or by any electronic, mechanical, or other means, now known or hereafter invented, including photocopying and recording, or in any information storage or retrieval system, without permission in writing from the publishers.

British Library Cataloguing in Publication Data
A catalogue record for this book is available from the British Library

Library of Congress Cataloging in Publication Data

ADELPHI series
ISSN 1944-5571

ADELPHI 430–431
ISBN 978-0-415-64487-7

Contents

Acknowledgements   9

Glossary   11

Introduction   13
Idealism   17
Realism   19
Pluralism   21
Stakes   23

Chapter One   **Power and restraint in American history**   31
The conservative anxiety   42
Cycles of ambition   49
Moments of restraint   57

Chapter Two   **Barack Obama and the limits of superpower**   71
Afghanistan   74
America: offshore balancer?   86
Humanitarian war   96
Counter-proliferation   101

Chapter Three   **Politics, polarisation and American exceptionalism**   111
Tea and liberty   112
Contested exceptionalism   115
Fiscal paralysis   123
Money and morals   131

Chapter Four   **The causes and consequences of austerity**   137
The road to ruin   139
Austerity politics   144
Balance and imbalance   151
Power shift?   155

Chapter Five   **Power, influence and leadership**   165
A world without followers   169
When coordination breaks down   174
Frustration and hubris   180

Conclusion   **Realist Dilemmas**   183
The plurality of power   190
The primacy of politics   196

Appendix   **American power in decline?**   199

Notes   205

ACKNOWLEDGEMENTS

The questions at the heart of this book were posed to the IISS by Disque and Carol Deane and Robert James. We gratefully acknowledge the intellectual enthusiasm, considerable patience and generous support of Mr and Mrs Deane and of the Robert and Ardis James Foundation. The answers, tentative as they may be, were made possible by some talented and dedicated research assistants. Special thanks go to Valeria Calderoni for her help in the final stages chasing down references, fact checking and commenting more generally. Along the way, Christoph Allin, Sophie Allin, Dina Esfandiary, Matthew Harries and Anna van Hollen helped with various chapters.

Some of the material in these pages was developed as the conversation progressed. Parts of chapters One, Two and Four are adapted from 'De Gaulle and American Power', in Benjamin M. Rowland (ed.), *Charles De Gaulle's Legacy of Ideas* (Lexington Books, 2011), 'US Policy and Afghanistan', in Toby Dodge and Nicholas Redman (eds) *Afghanistan to 2015 and Beyond* (Routledge for IISS, 2011), pp. 47–68, 'United States: Broken Consensus', in *Strategic Survey 2011: The Annual Review of World Affairs* (Routledge for IISS, 2011), pp. 139–59, 'As Good as It Gets?', *Survival*, vol. 53, no. 3 (June–July 2011) pp. 205–15. Chapter Five draws upon material from 'Elusive Power, Essential Leadership', *Survival*, vol. 51, no. 3, (June–July 2009) pp. 243–51; 'A Great Fall,' *Survival*, vol. 52, no. 4 (August–September 2010) pp. 177–82; 'European Security, Transatlantic Relations, and the Challenge to U.S. Global Leadership', in Riccardo Alcaro and Erik Jones (eds), *European Security and the Future of Transatlantic Relations* (Edizioni Nuova Cultura, 2011), pp. 149–68; and 'Power, Leadership, and U.S. Foreign Policy', *International Spectator*, vol. 46, no. 3 (September 2011), pp. 19–29.

Our thinking over many years about America's world role has been refined through conversation, debate and the eloquent writings of many colleagues. From the start, David Calleo and John Harper have been cherished friends and steady mentors. In addition for this project, John Chipman, Nigel Inkster, Alexander Nicoll, Jeffrey Mazo, Christian Le Mière, James Hackett, Mark Fitzpatrick, John Buck, Michael Palliser, Thomas Row, Giri Rajendran, Steve Simon, David Unger and Adam Ward read chapters, provided advice or acted as essential sounding boards. We also benefitted from the wider network available to us through SAIS and the IISS. Janis Lee and Nick Redman were talented, scrupulous and patient editors. Though it may go without saying, it is worth repeating: errors of fact or interpretation are ours alone.

GLOSSARY

AIPAC	The American Israel Public Affairs Committee
CENTCOM	US Central Command
FHLMC (Freddie Mac)	Federal Home Loan Mortgage Corporation
FNMA (Fannie Mae)	Federal National Mortgage Association
GDP	Gross Domestic Product
IMF	International Monetary Fund
NATO	North Atlantic Treaty Organisation
SEAL	United States navy's Sea, Air, and Land teams
S&P	Standard & Poor's credit-rating agency
TARP	Troubled Asset Relief Program

To my mother, Evelyn Hansen Allin, and to my father, John Allin

*   *   *

To my parents, Hanne and Sydney Jones

On 1 December 2009, near the end of his first year in office, President Barack Obama travelled to the US Military Academy at West Point, New York, to announce the deployment of another 30,000 troops to Afghanistan. The president's speech followed a difficult and bruising inter-agency debate among participants from the White House, the Pentagon, the State Department and intelligence agencies on whether to expand the Afghanistan war into a fully resourced counter-insurgency campaign, or – in effect – to cut American losses by reverting to a narrower, targeted campaign of attrition against Islamist terrorists based mainly in Pakistan.

By escalating, Obama appeared to be siding with the more ambitious counter-insurgency advocates. But this appearance was possibly deceiving. For his speech at West Point contained striking notes of caution, restraint and limits – limits of both time and purpose – regarding the American mission in Afghanistan. He told the cadets:

As president, I refuse to set goals that go beyond
our responsibility, our means, or our interests. And
I must weigh all of the challenges that our nation
faces. I don't have the luxury of committing to just
one. Indeed, I'm mindful of the words of President
Eisenhower, who – in discussing our national security – said: 'each proposal must be weighed in the
light of a broader consideration: the need to maintain balance in and among national programs'.[1]

The Eisenhower quotation was a telling expression of
Obama's small-c conservatism, characterised by a concern
with restoring a balance between international commitments
on the one hand, and American capabilities and resources on
the other. Over the course of Obama's first term, the administration has undertaken a degree of strategic retrenchment.
It has made good on Obama's promise to withdraw from
Iraq, started to draw down in Afghanistan, outlined modest
but still significant cuts to defence spending, put the United
Kingdom and France ostentatiously to the fore as leaders
of a NATO intervention in Libya, and signalled a strategic
'pivot' from land wars in the Middle East to what some
analysts described as an 'offshore balancing' posture relying
on naval and air power and on regional allies.

The retrenchment comes in the midst of a global
economic crisis, with attendant pressures for budgetary
austerity. Cutting government spending, including defence
spending, during a savage economic slump is not a rational
short-term response to the collapse of economic demand.
The long-term pressures on US government spending are

real enough, however, and tied to the overall strength of the US economy. 'Over the past several years,' said Obama in the same West Point speech, '[we've] failed to appreciate the connection between our national security and our economy.' From the outset of their administration, moreover, the president and his advisers took pains to emphasise the relationship between current and future resources and various kinds of deficits: a fiscal deficit and strategic over-commitment embodied in two wars; a moral deficit embodied in the George W. Bush administration's official sanction of torture, Abu Ghraib, Guantanamo, the invasion of Iraq and close ally Israel's occupation of the West Bank; and an attention deficit caused by the United States' over-commitment in the Middle East – to the detriment of other interests and concerns, especially the key strategic theatre of the Asia-Pacific.

There are cycles to American ambitions in the world. The current sense of American overstretch and exhaustion in some respects seems reminiscent of the 1960s and early 1970s, a time of deepening realisation that the Vietnam War was a strategic quagmire. It was during the process of the Vietnam escalation that the Southern Democratic Senator J. William Fulbright decried what he saw as 'the arrogance of those who would make America the world's policeman'.[2] Fulbright's *cri de coeur* was the prelude to a period of fierce and sometimes violent national polarisation about many things, including America's proper global role.

In the current phase we have not seen the mass demonstration, riots or domestic terrorism that the US experienced in the late 1960s and early 1970s. In other respects, however, the American body politic seems even more polarised today than it was in Fulbright's time. As the president proposes to reconfigure US strategy, the Republican candidates for president, including Mitt Romney (at the time of writing the presumptive nominee), label him a practised 'appeaser'. If Romney becomes president in 2013, he will probably be constrained by the same economic austerity and general war-weariness as that which has affected Obama. Nonetheless, Romney and other Republicans do not acknowledge – at least not explicitly – that America became overstretched in the first decade of the twenty-first century, and they have promised an aggressive and unapologetic re-assertion of America's pre-eminent place in the world.[3] Obama, for his part, is hardly proposing that America withdraw from its global responsibilities. Obama's America would not abdicate the policeman's role, though it might pursue narrower ambitions and would certainly try, as in the 2011 Libyan operation, to enlist others to join and sometimes even lead the force.

What are America's real responsibilities, real limitations and real options as a world power in the twenty-first century? The options can be explored in the context of a long-standing and ongoing debate involving three different categories of arguments. One category is idealistic and expansionist; it rests on the belief that the United States must lead because it is the only power with the capabilities and values to do so. A second is more pragmatic or realist; it argues that American leadership should be by example, where possible, and should focus more narrowly on the national interest where there is any requirement to resort to force. A third is more limited and more pluralist; it insists that the United States act only sparingly, and that it should retrench in its commitments both to replenish its resources against uncertain future requirements and to adapt to the challenge of promoting collective action in a more multi-polar world.

These voices often overlap and intermingle. When we start assigning them to real people, we find that many speak from different perspectives at the same time. Nevertheless, it is important to sketch out these logical types if only to make sense of the conversation taking place.

Idealism

When Robert Kagan published his *Policy Review* essay on 'Power and Weakness', he crystallised the presumption that the United States must police the world because it is uniquely competent to do so.[4] Kagan's constituted an important idealist argument not least because it offered a plausible secular case for American 'exceptionalism'. The United States, according to Kagan, was more likely than its European allies to pursue military solutions to global security problems, not due to innate cultural or moral differences, but because America's immensely greater military capacities conditioned the national psychology about when it was proper and useful to employ force.

In other writings, Kagan has emphasised American historical traditions that make it a natural champion of universal liberty.[5] But it was Kagan's key insight that the 'exceptional' role of America in the world had structural, more than moral or cultural, causes. That role also had positive moral consequences, he contended, because the world was a dangerous place that required a benign hegemon ready to use military force. The European Union, a 'postmodern' paradise of law and peaceful integration, constituted a triumph of human progress – a 'blessed miracle' in Kagan's formulation – but this miracle was only possible because the United States stood ready as global security guarantor.

This argument was well-suited to its moment. Writing in the summer of 2002, Kagan not only tapped a rich vein of American self-confidence coming off the successful campaign against the Taliban government in Afghanistan, but also the widespread frustration with perceived European foot-dragging in dealing with Saddam Hussein. More importantly, perhaps, Kagan's argument was neither exclusively Republican nor even essentially right-wing.

President Obama's rhetoric about America's global responsibilities is not far removed from the Kagan version of exceptionalism. Other Democrats have made similar claims, most obviously when their party controlled the White House. Then Secretary of State Madeleine Albright's assertion that the United States is the 'indispensable nation' is a good example.[6] Like Kagan's, Albright's claim resonated with the moment. Americans were bouncing from the success of the 1995 Dayton Peace Accords to the ultimatum implicit in the 1999 negotiations at Rambouillet. Despite the scandal that beset President Bill Clinton, American self-confidence in the world was high. Moreover, many Americans were frustrated with perceived European fecklessness in dealing with Slobodan Milosevic as Yugoslavia disintegrated.

Kagan and Albright came to the same conclusion but from different intellectual starting points. Kagan is an intellectual who reanimated and redefined neo-conservatism.[7] Albright comes from a more classical realist tradition, albeit one interwoven with a strong commitment to the preservation of international norms and the protection of human rights. They both came to believe that the United States had a unique combination of attributes – the ability to distinguish between right and wrong, the capability to influence events on the ground, and the responsibility to make things happen. Europeans have a hard time understanding how anyone can have such delusions of omnipotence. American adherents to this worldview respond by pointing to what might have happened if the United States were not around.

Realism

Not everyone shares that perspective. Former national security adviser Brent Scowcroft has emerged as an icon of a more restrained interpretation of America's world role. Drawing upon his experience in the George H.W. Bush administration, he has argued consistently that the United States should avoid overt triumphalism, that it should husband its resources and discriminate when picking fights.[8] Such modesty has its roots in America's failure to predict the end of the Cold War and in the recognition that cooperation with the Soviets was crucial in bringing about the transition to post-communism. Scowcroft was a principal in the decision not to capture Baghdad during the first Gulf War as well. He was conscious of the US' power to overthrow Saddam Hussein but equally aware of the huge degree of uncertainty surrounding such an action and the costly commitment it would likely entail.

Realism, in this rendering, should not be confused with the school of international-relations theory that goes by the same name. Realism, rather, is a foreign-policy attitude and proclivity. It is mindful of American limits, of the dangers of over-extension, and the problem of unintended consequences. Though he sometimes espouses a version of exceptionalist idealism, President Obama also fits the realist category, and when he ran for president he expressed admiration for the foreign-policy realism of Scowcroft and other members of the George H.W. Bush administration, including James Baker and Colin Powell. Richard Nixon and Henry Kissinger were accomplished American realists in this sense – the opening to China being their great realist achievement.

The contemporary argument for American foreign-policy realism extends beyond the strictly material domain of power politics. Hence realists such as Scowcroft recognise that the United States can deploy a wide arsenal of power resources. The 'soft power' argument promulgated in Joseph Nye's writings is one illustration; Samuel Huntington's *Clash of Civilisations* is another.[9] The distinction between these examples is that, whereas Nye has emphasised the powerful forms of attraction embedded in the American economic and social model, Huntington forced us to consider that other models may have attractions of their own.

The idealism of the neoconservatives close to the George W. Bush administration drowned out the voices of realism soon after Islamic fundamentalists attacked New York and Washington on 11 September 2001. The attacks were seized upon to argue that the threat to American security was existential. All that remained was for the most dangerous people to gain access to the most dangerous weapons; as then Vice President Dick Cheney insisted, even a 1% probability of such an outcome would be unacceptable.[10]

Realists had to wait until the passion of the moment had settled and the United States woke up to a vastly expanded set of foreign military commitments. Then Secretary of State Colin Powell was the manifestation of that predicament. He warned all along that 'you own it if you break it' and yet he could do little to dissuade an administration determined to uphold its ideals and to follow its convictions.[11]

The realist perspective continued to evolve in the shadow of 9/11 and through the recent history of global economic turmoil. Meanwhile, the focus narrowed down to how the United States can get the most leverage out of the assets at its disposal. Hence, for example, the 'smart power' commission organised by the Center for Strategic and International Studies brought together realists from all parts of the US foreign-policy community, including Nye and Powell's State Department deputy, Richard Armitage.[12] The Princeton Project on National Security, led by G. John Ikenberry and Anne-Marie Slaughter, ploughs the same furrow.[13] The conclusion of both groups was that the United States should act flexibly within its constraints in order to make the most of its global leadership. This was the ethos that was adopted by the Obama administration.

Pluralism

The question is whether flexibility is enough to avoid a creeping over-commitment. Many of Obama's critics both on the right and on the left believe it is not. Their reasoning is that both idealists and realists in American foreign-policy debates underestimate the scope of the changes taking place in the world. The perspective here is informed less by the experience of a single lifetime in public policy and more by a healthy respect for much longer-running dynamics. Paul Kennedy's 1987 *Rise and Fall of Great Powers* is the best-known expression of this perspective.[14] His analysis of diplomatic history over five centuries in Western Europe suggests a logic of overstretch that is almost inevitable.

According to this pluralist view, the natural distribution of power in the world is inevitably plural. American hegemony is unnatural, unsustainable and corrosive to both the American domestic political economy and the international system. Imperial pretensions are dangerous, and even if a degree of American 'exceptionalism' is acknowledged, it is not seen to diminish that danger. In addition to Kennedy, the pluralists have included George F. Kennan, Charles de Gaulle, David Calleo and Robert Skidelsky. Pluralists are highly attentive to economic power and may have a greater tendency to discount military power. Hence, the fact that the European Union has long been an economic peer of the United States is accorded greater significance by David Calleo than it is by Robert Kagan.

Within this perspective, the challenge is not to avoid decline, but rather to manage it. A succession of books stretching back to Calleo's *America and the World Political Economy* (co-authored with Benjamin Rowland) and Robert Gilpin's *U.S. Power and the Multinational Corporation* suggest how this may be accomplished.[15] Such writers argue for a recalibration of alliance politics and a reconsideration of free-market economics. They believe other countries should be required to shoulder much of the burden of world order – even if this means that some countries must be allowed to fail in these enterprises. And they are much more interested in the distribution of benefits from international commerce than they are persuaded by the nostrum that liberalisation enhances welfare for the world writ large.

This perspective is not an abdication of American leadership. Rather, it is a call for the United States to expend the energy required to lead only where it matters most, lest American leadership should allow other countries to become dependent upon having easy access to American power as a resource. Indeed, by withholding security and forcing other countries to look out for their own interests, the US government not only slows the process of creeping over-commitment, but also exercises a form of influence that otherwise would not be available.

Stakes

The long-historical sweep of the so-called 'declinist' argument is both a strength and a shortcoming. It is a strength insofar as it has forced all voices in the debate about America's world role to reflect on the lessons of history. It is a weakness insofar as the more distant consequences of decline are so easily overshadowed by current events. Urgency and importance do not always fit on the same scale. When Muammar Gadhafi threatened to slaughter protesters in Benghazi in 2011, what mattered was the prospect that, unless decisive action was taken, a large number of civilians would be wiped out. The long-run consequences of creeping over-commitment pale significantly in such a context.

Even less obvious 'ticking bomb' situations can have a similar effect of focusing attention on the present, whatever the lessons of the past. Indeed, the pluralist argument only gets a full hearing when the long-run future suddenly looks imminent. The relative ascendance of Germany and Europe in the late 1960s and early 1970s focused popular attention on the declinist thesis; the rise of Japan in the 1980s tightened the focus again; the sudden emergence in the early twenty-first century of China as a major economic power triggered a third wave of declinist concern.

The threat that most easily grabs American attention is the threat to prosperity rather than security. The shock of terrorist attacks on New York and Washington on 9/11 was unusual in this regard. Most Americans accept that the United States is the pre-eminent military power and few imagine that a rival in Europe, Asia or elsewhere will rise up to challenge that dominance. Rogue states may take control over weapons of mass destruction; terrorist groups may perform random acts of violence; and conflicts between other countries, such as Israel and Iran, for example, could threaten vital American concerns. But such developments would not constitute the rise of a security challenger comparable, for example, to Nazi Germany or the Soviet Union.

Economic challenges are more plausible than threats to American military predominance and, in many ways, even self-evident. They can be seen in the transfer of manufacturing jobs overseas. They are implicit in the growth of sovereign wealth funds and foreign-held US government debt. And they manifest in unprecedented current-account deficits and in the ubiquitous 'made in China' or 'made in Japan' labels attached to consumer goods. The economic and financial crisis that set in with such ferocity in 2007 and 2008 may not have created the sense of economic apprehension, but it certainly exacerbated it. It also strengthened suspicions that efforts to safeguard US prosperity would depend upon a reconsideration of the country's world role.

Whenever there is an open debate about American decline, there is a debate about globalisation lurking in the background: prosperity and security are inextricably interconnected. This is true in straightforward terms of guns and butter or technological superiority, but it is evident in the soft-power context as well. The wealth of the United States is an important source of its attraction for the rest of the world. It is a principal achievement of the American political and social model. And it legitimates a faith in free markets, which other countries might otherwise view as too inequitable.

In turn, the attraction of the American economic and social model makes it easier for the United States to convince other countries to cooperate. If they work with the US, they may share in American prosperity. American prosperity makes it more likely that other countries will contribute to American security as well. The Atlantic Alliance was founded on the Marshall Plan and not just the rejection of communism. It implied a 'compromise of embedded liberalism' in which countries were encouraged to pursue their own domestic priorities within a cooperative international regime.[16]

By extension, anything that undermines American economic prosperity affects American security by chipping away at its global leadership. The end of prosperity is also *The End of Influence,* as argued in a 2010 book by Stephen Cohen and J. Bradford DeLong.[17] And without influence, the United States is more likely to find itself acting alone. This means that if American prosperity is being undermined by a creeping over-commitment abroad, the problem is more likely to worsen than it is to correct itself. The more American prosperity is weakened, the more difficulty the US will face bringing other countries along with it and the more likely it will be to overextend itself abroad. Cooperation gives way to competition, and competition has little to offer in dealing with violent conflict. Hence, a United States committed to its own global leadership may find itself caught in a vicious circle. The more it tries to act as the global policeman, the more it will damage its very ability to carry out that role.

*   *   *

All three perspectives are valid expressions of historical realities and core American traditions. Any American president will be challenged to shape a version of American leadership that respects the constraints of this three-way argument between idealists, realists and pluralists. The resulting policies should respect and maintain the United States' unique capacity to promote security and world order; it should make intelligent use of America's many different capabilities and assets; and it should avoid doing damage to the economic prosperity that is 'the wellspring' of American power.[18]

The Obama administration's approach to Afghanistan and Libya suggests how this new strategy for American leadership might evolve. While the Obama administration has made progress in redefining a more sustainable world role, it has also uncovered significant vulnerabilities in its initial strategy which need to be given thorough consideration. The American people can appreciate economic constraints, but they have a hard time connecting those constraints to the effects on US global leadership, and they are also confused by the inability of the Obama administration to bring other important international actors along. This is a potent source of criticism. More than ever in recent memory, the success of US foreign policy depends upon the performance of other countries. The scale of its interdependence is much greater and the sensitivity of its domestic policy to failure is heightened as well. Hence, while Obama's approach should be praised, there are grounds for caution in that other countries will have to play their part if the United States is to succeed in redefining its world role.

It is useful for our purposes to offer a brief overview of the current debate, in which there are three dominant themes: redistribution, restraint and restoration.

The argument about redistribution centres on China, but can be extended to include any number of emerging powers. Fareed Zakaria and Thomas Friedman are among the best known contributors to the line of analysis, whereby these new powers will fundamentally reshape world order.[19] Yet it would be careless to presume that one or more of these newly emergent powers will assume the mantle of global hegemony. China is the obvious candidate, but others could be mooted.[20] The problem is that none of the imagined new superpowers is either interested or able to assume the role once played by the United States. This suggests that no-one will take responsibility for the global system; world order will collapse down to a G-zero in Ian Bremmer's terminology or, as Charles Kupchan puts it, it will become no-one's world.[21]

Of course, leadership is not the same as order and the structures created by the United States when it was relatively more powerful continue to guide interaction at the global level. This is the point made most powerfully by G. John Ikenberry, but it has a pedigree stretching back to Robert Keohane and before.[22] Ikenberry suggests that 'the underlying principles of liberal international order' will survive, and that the United States could be able to renegotiate 'for an ongoing leadership role in the management of the system'.[23] The concern raised by this argument is whether the United States retains the resources to play even this more modest role. This is where the issue of restraint becomes important.

The relative decline of the United States coincided with a tightening of constraints on the country's material wealth. The US economy is not only losing its predominance in terms of domestic output, but it also has much weaker claims on the rest of the world's wealth.[24] The implication, as Michael Mandelbaum argues, is that the US government no longer has the ability to provide unlimited public goods at the global level; it must make difficult decisions about the composition and use of the US military as well; and it must balance these claims against other more purely domestic concerns.[25] Moreover, as the constraints on the US economy have tightened, the ability of the US political system to act decisively has diminished.[26] Its international competitiveness has weakened.[27] And its influence in the rest of the world has waned.[28]

This debate about the restraints on American resources has shaken the country to its core. It challenges not only American self-conceptions but also more traditional notions of power. In the past, the United States was always able to rise to the challenge, so perhaps it can adapt to this latest redistribution of global power.[29] The notion of inexorable decline, Kagan argues, is based on an unsound extrapolation of the current economic crisis.[30] Moreover, the US possesses a wide range of assets that stretch beyond physical resources and industrial innovation to include a fundamentally and universally appealing way of life. These are the building blocks of Joseph Nye's 'soft power'. Such attributes should not be so easily degraded or overshadowed. The power of American ideas and ideals should continue to shine. The challenge is to rediscover the determination and self-confidence that are essential to American global leadership.[31]

Here is where the doctrine of restoration, as Richard Haass called it in a recent issue of *The American Interest*, becomes important.[32] The basic idea is one that is already central to the policies of Barack Obama's administration. Yet for it to succeed, the United States must decide to make a determined effort. This requires more than just a simple assertion of American exceptionalism or a claim to the uniqueness of America's world role. It requires a clear calculation of priorities.[33] The most important is to strengthen the domestic economy – which is the 'wellspring' of American power.[34]

The critical element in this restoration theme is how the United States shares responsibility with other significant actors at the global level. If the United States is to restore its leadership, then it will have to restore both its authority and its legitimacy as well. The reality is that too many of the problems to be faced are too large for the United States to tackle alone. The United States must mobilise other countries to work with it, or it will over-reach is resources, sacrifice its credibility and ultimately fail. This prospect is what sets out the real stakes in the debate.

CHAPTER ONE

Power and restraint in American history

On 13 December 1847, from Washington, the first-term Congressman Abraham Lincoln wrote to his law partner back in Illinois: 'As you are all so anxious for me to distinguish myself, I have concluded to do so, before long.' The young Lincoln fulfilled this undertaking by introducing in the House of Representatives a resolution demanding of President James Polk some confirmation that the clash between American and Mexican troops that started the Mexican–American war had indeed taken place, as the President claimed, on American soil. Lincoln soon backed another resolution declaring that the war had been 'unnecessarily and unconstitutionally' started by the United States. The following spring Lincoln wrote: '[i]t is a fact that the United States Army, in marching to the Rio Grande, marched into a peaceful Mexican settlement, and frightened the inhabitants away from their homes and their growing crops.'[1]

The challenges from Lincoln and a few fellow Whigs against America's Mexican adventure were doubly quixotic:

firstly, because the fighting was already over by the time they were issued; and secondly, because the war and its fruit, a vast expansion of American territory, were extremely popular among aroused American patriots. For historian John L. Harper, the Mexican–American war (1846–48) was the archetypal case of a now all-too-familiar event: one of 'America's unnecessary wars.'[2] For Robert Kagan, however, the conflict with Mexico can be identified as a key moment of demonstration that this 'dangerous nation', the United States, meant business.[3] Kagan does not sugar-coat the nature of the war – he recognises that an important consequence and principle motive for it was to expand Southern 'slave power' in its continuing political struggle with the 'Free States' of the North. But neither does Kagan believe that the impulse that gave rise to it can be isolated from the wellsprings of American greatness or its mission in the wider world. Kagan's broader argument is that America, a nation-state pursuing national interests in a similar fashion as other nation states, has nonetheless conceived those interests in terms that served human liberty more often than they harmed it. Although undeniably accompanied by its share of humbug and cant, it was this 'universalistic nationalism', in Kagan's words, that put America in a position to play the necessary role of world's policeman.[4]

Other prerequisites included the consolidation of the American federal construction around a central authority, and a settlement of the slavery question. Both projects were accomplished, of course, by the same Abraham Lincoln, who thereby proved – to put it in the vernacular of a later age – that he did not oppose all wars, just stupid ones. The Civil War erupted because the Northern strategy of containing – rather than destroying – the evil of slavery proved unsustainable. Lincoln famously maintained that he would have accepted a compromise that left the Union, and therefore also slavery, intact, so long as slavery's geographical limits could likewise be maintained. But Lincoln's war, as it dragged on for five bloody years, transmuted into something more unforgiving and absolute: a crusade against slavery, with the profound nobility and sustained cruelty that crusades so often carry This crusading conviction – which drew on the beliefs set out in Thomas Jefferson's Declaration of Independence and was radically reinterpreted in Lincoln's Gettysburg Address in 1863[5] – was to infuse the American global imperialism that gained momentum in the twentieth century (following the continental imperialism of the nineteenth century). One could not say of twentieth-century America, as John Quincy Adams had said of his country in 1821, that it would 'go not abroad, in search of monsters to destroy'.[6]

Kagan's might be labelled the 'warts and all' argument. Global liberty and global security need a powerful champion, but one cannot expect that champion to be anything better than an imperfect political animal, with feet of clay. The argument can be explored by way of an historical counter-factual. What if Lincoln's America had purified itself not through civil war, but by allowing the Confederate South to secede? Benefits are not hard to imagine. Most obviously, the bloodiest war (for Americans) in American history might have been avoided. Southern slavery, presumably, would have withered away within a decade or two in any event, as it had withered elsewhere. The Northern, Midwestern and

Western United States might have emerged in the twentieth century as a more coherent political entity more comfortably allied with European social democracies. Though one cannot assume there would have been effortless racial harmony in the North, it is fair to say that the millstone of segregation would not have so damaged the American effort to promote Western values during the early Cold War. Today's bitter cultural, political and constitutional antagonisms would be far less salient without the continued North–South polarisation to drive them

And yet, a smaller United States would have been, in important respects, a weaker United States. It is hard to see America without the Southern states having had the military and productive capacity to rise to the occasion of the Second World War.[7] That 'necessary war' constituted the moment when American industrial and military power arrived as the decisive factor for allied victory and for shaping the post-war order. Others, notably the Soviet Union, suffered far greater losses, without which Nazi Germany would not have been defeated, but it was America that tipped the balance. Hence, following Kagan's logic, the war to re-conquer the South eight decades earlier was necessary to make America a great world power. So too, in fact, were the acquisitions of Texas, New Mexico, Arizona, Nevada, Utah and California.[8] The Mexican War and the American Civil War – a 'bad war' and a 'good' one in Lincoln's terms – were both unavoidable steps on the way to American global hegemony. And that hegemony was indispensable, for a global power was needed to replace the exhausted British Empire. Kagan has argued:

It is too easily forgotten that the plans for world order devised by American policy-makers in the early 1940s were not aimed at containing the Soviet Union, which many of them still viewed as a potential partner. Rather, those policy-makers were looking backward to the circumstances that had led to the catastrophe of global war. Their purpose was to construct a more stable international order than the one that collapsed in the 1930s: an economic system that furthered the aim of international stability by promoting growth and free trade; and a framework for international security that, although it placed some faith in the ability of the great powers to work together, rested ultimately on the keystone of American power.[9]

The interwar crises, and then the cataclysm of the Second World War itself, shaped the imperialist-cum-idealist convictions of a generation of American strategists. The collapse of world order had coincided with the decline of pax Britannica, and so its replacement by a new pax Americana was considered the only viable alternative to international anarchy.

This idea developed over time. John Harper narrated the early-twentieth-century debate about America's world role as an argument between Woodrow Wilson and Theodore Roosevelt (TR), with Theodore's distant cousin Franklin oscillating – both socially and ideologically – between the two camps.[10] Today's debates carry faint echoes of the arguments between Wilson and TR a century ago. Woodrow Wilson certainly handed down a legacy of idealism to both modern liberals and neoconservatives. But his actual presidency was constrained by events. Germany's blunder of unrestricted submarine warfare brought the US into the First World War, yet Wilson was reasonably consistent in imagining that the United States would fight not to vindicate French and British aims, but to replace their system of power with something better and more durable: peace without victory. In practice, of course, America joined in an allied victory that contained the humiliations, impoverishment and embitterment of Germany's people against which Wilson had warned.

Theodore Roosevelt derided Wilson's ideas of supplanting and transcending a balance of power as foolish and naive. A devotee of naval strategist Alfred Thayer Mahan, TR believed that the United States should support British naval power as the first line of America's own defence. In this, Teddy Roosevelt could be considered a realist, but he also insisted, in terms that resonate for today's neoconservatives, that a big problem with Wilson's vision was its moral murkiness and failure to discern the civilisational superiority of imperial Britain over the Kaiser's Germany. Both Wilson and TR were progressives at home (though only Roosevelt acknowledged the evils of segregation). But Roosevelt, unlike Wilson, seemed not to worry that military deployments abroad would threaten social and political progress at home.[11] (In the event, of course, it was Wilson who presided over a wartime administration that implemented draconian curbs on Americans' civil liberties.)

Franklin Delano Roosevelt (FDR) consciously emulated his cousin, the national hero TR, and served as assistant secretary of the navy in the administration of Teddy's bitter rival Wilson. Like TR, FDR nurtured a hearty dislike for modern Germany (though, with many Americans of his class and generation, he had a nostalgic affection for the dying vestiges of a pre-Bismarkian, Gothic and pastoral Germany that he had visited in his youth). Like Wilson, however, FDR was at best ambivalent about British power and society. He obviously worked intimately and well with Winston Churchill to manage the Second World War. To Churchill's huge dismay, however, FDR made no secret of his hope and expectation that the war would bring about the demise of the British Empire. This was in keeping with FDR's generally disdainful view of the old European powers and their future. As Harper has put it:

> The one truly profound conviction that linked Roosevelt to Wilson was that Europe constituted the overriding problem of the twentieth century and that the United States had little choice but to try to solve it ... Both Wilson and FDR were inclined to believe – and the World War tended to confirm – that the New World was morally superior to the Old World and that the future belonged to the dynamic, healthy elements of civilisation led by the United States. What linked FDR to Wilson was the notion that the rest of humanity must be saved from Europe, and Europe from itself.[12]

The way in which FDR melded the perspectives of Wilson and TR is captured in John Lewis Gaddis's assessment of the 'four policemen' directorate, an arguably eccentric FDR concept – comprising the United States, Russia, Britain and China. This became, with the addition of France, the core permanent membership of the UN Security Council. The four policemen would work by power politics and alliance machination as much as by consensus: America, Russia and China sometimes against Imperial Britain; America, Britain and China sometimes against Russia. 'The picture is hardly one of anticipating harmony,' Gaddis has written.[13]

For thinking about America's twenty-first century role, what is perhaps most interesting about FDR's vision was its limits. An American policeman was to be required – but FDR saw the United States as only one of four, implying a degree of regional pluralism or, at least, realist wariness of foreign entanglements. Roosevelt was a great politician and a successful wartime leader, but his post-war vision when he died was, at best, half-formed. Still, we can infer a world in which Russia and China enjoyed considerable sway over Eurasia, Britain maintained at least shared naval supremacy with the United States, and the US would withdraw its troops from Europe, reverting to a posture of off-shore balancer: a global power ready to defend its interests in many places while becoming entangled in as few as possible. In current American discourse, the posture would probably be labelled 'isolationist'. And Harper describes the worldview of one important faction in Roosevelt's administration as 'Europhobic hemispherism'[14] under which America could continue to enjoy some tangible benefit from its geographical position. 'Isolationism', along with 'appeasement', have become such careless epithets as to lose most of their analytical value. That the man who led America through the Second World War could be considered, in today's terminology, both an isolationist and an appeaser does indicate, however, how expectations of American power have grown.

*   *   *

FDR's vision of the post-war order did not come to pass. Stalin's brutality in Eastern Europe demolished American hopes for serious post-war cooperation with the Soviet ally. Washington then had to reappraise its world role. The sudden death of Roosevelt served to punctuate, if not precipitate, this reappraisal. Men like Harry Truman and Dean Acheson emerged as champions of the idea that world order required America to be the keystone.

Since Acheson stands out as America's archetypal liberal hawk, it is worth remembering that his hardline views were shaped gradually. A first-generation Anglo-American, he was, before and during the war, essentially Victorian in outlook, committed to the restoration of a nineteenth-century system that had sustained the halcyon world into which he came of age. As Britain weakened, the New Englander Acheson did not so much imagine America replacing it as joining in permanent partnership with it. He was a free-trader who nonetheless accepted the need for Britain to maintain some of its imperial trading arrangements, and he became a partial convert to Keynesianism (from his initial austere, sound-money rectitude), partly because of circumstances, but also because of a necessary working relationship and ensuing friendship with Keynes himself. This was before Keynes's fatal heart attack, when he was struggling beyond exhaustion against Washington's inclination to treat Britain's debt and the flow of funds across the Atlantic in ways that rendered the UK practically bankrupt. Acheson was not congenitally anti-Soviet either. He worked well with the Russians during and for some time after the war, not easily giving up hopes for reconciling the growing differences between Washington and Moscow.[15]

Acheson's anti-Soviet epiphany coincided with the realisation that a full British partnership was not available. In the freezing penury of February 1947, London's announcement that it would have to terminate aid to Turkey and Greece thrust a new crisis upon the crisis-weary Truman administration. Acheson and his colleagues pushed for the United States to take on Britain's role in the eastern Mediterranean.[16] President Truman's aid request to a joint session of Congress on 12 March 1947 emphasised economic rather than military support, and in theory the requested $450 million could be seen as a down-payment on the $13 billion Marshall Plan for Europe that was to be initiated four months later. An economic programme to restore European commerce and confidence could be seen, in turn, as a plan for America to help restore a European and global balance of power, allowing it to then substantially withdraw. Such was certainly the intention of a principle Marshall Plan architect, George F. Kennan, who was then the State Department's Director of Policy Planning. Yet Truman's initial aid request for Greece and Turkey was wrapped in what became a much grander

Truman Doctrine. 'I believe,' he told Congress, 'that it must be the policy of the United States to support free peoples who are resisting attempted subjugation by armed minorities or by outside pressures.'[17] This, an alarmed Kennan would later write, 'placed our aid to Greece in the framework of a universal policy rather than in that of a specific decision addressed to a specific set of circumstances.'[18] Such universalism, in Kennan's view, became an American habit with baleful consequences:

> Throughout the ensuing two decades the conduct of our foreign policy would continue to be bedevilled by people in our own government as well as in other governments who could not free themselves from the belief that all another country had to do, in order to qualify for American aid, was to demonstrate the existence of a Communist threat. Since almost no country was without a communist minority, this assumption carried very far.[19]

Two years after Truman's speech, Washington made the clear choice not just to restore a European and global balance of power, but to assume responsibility for managing it. The Truman administration established NATO in April 1949 as a standing, peacetime military alliance, and a year after that it promulgated, in a Report to the National Security Council (NSC68), a plan for American rearmament and aggressive containment of Soviet power. A few months later, when North Korean troops moved south across the 38th parallel, the American policeman went to work.

The conservative anxiety

There is room for debate on how the eighteenth-century founders of the American republic conceived its future world role – not least because the founders debated it among themselves. Washington vowed to 'steer clear of permanent alliance' and Jefferson said much the same about the dangers of 'entangling alliances'. Yet the same Jefferson took the opportunity in 1803 to realise his vision of an American 'empire of liberty' as soon as he had the chance, by purchasing the territory of Louisiana (more than 820,000 square miles) from Napoleon.[20] And, for all the American pretentions of isolation from Europe's conflicts, the Napoleonic wars (1799–1815) were a deeply polarising current in American politics, so the question was not whether to align but rather, with whom? This was one of the many disagreements, for example between Alexander Hamilton and his bitter rival Jefferson (the Francophile and French Revolution enthusiast). Hamilton sought a tacit alliance with Great Britain, as a stepping stone to world power.[21]

What is more certain, however, is that the drafters of the US constitution worried that wartime concentrations of power in an American executive could pose a threat to republican liberty. James Madison gave voice to this worry at the Constitutional Convention of 1787:

> In time of actual war, great discretionary powers are constantly given to the Executive Magistrate. Constant apprehension of war has the same tendency to render the head too large for the body. A standing military force, with an overgrown Executive

will not long be safe companions to liberty. The means of defence against foreign danger, have been always the instruments of tyranny at home. Among the Romans it was a standing maxim to excite a war, whenever a revolt was apprehended. Throughout all Europe, the armies kept up under the pretext of defending, have enslaved the people.[22]

Similar concern for the proper constitutional limits to a president's powers fed much of the domestic anxiety about Cold War over-reach. Republican Senator Robert Taft, who had opposed with equal vigour Roosevelt's New Deal and pre-Pearl Harbour efforts to involve America in the war against Adolf Hitler, was also worried that post-war mobilising against Stalin would lead to a growth in the United States government and threaten American liberty far more than Stalin himself. (Taft went so far in his constitutional scruples as to embark on a Quixotic argument against the Nuremburg war-crimes tribunal: calling it victors' justice and a violation of the 'fundamental principle of American law that a man cannot be tried under an *ex post facto* statute'.)[23]

The most articulate and influential worrier about American overstretch was Kennan – though it bears emphasis that Kennan ultimately influenced debate and historiography more than US policy. It says something about their overlapping worldviews that Kennan, like Taft, considered Nuremburg a travesty. Kennan was appalled by the spectacle of American jurists sitting in judgment together with the man who had been chief Soviet prosecutor at the Moscow show trials in 1936 and 1937. While serving as a diplomat in Russia, a young Kennan had been required to sit through those trials, which had added to his own 'liberal education in the horrors of Stalinism', as he put it.[24] Reposted, late in the war, to the US embassy in Moscow, Kennan in February 1946 composed the 'Long Telegram' that made him famous – an 5,500-word manifesto against a Russian 'political force committed fanatically to the belief that with the US there can be no permanent *modus vivendi*, that it is desirable and necessary that the internal harmony of our society be disrupted, our traditional way of life be destroyed, the international authority of our state be broken, if Soviet power is to be secure.'[25]

Yet, although this manifesto would be remembered as a founding document in the American decision to wage Cold War, Kennan was always clear that America's commitment to this war should be limited. His vision of containment was mainly political and economic rather than military. He was opposed to the idea of NATO as an elaborate, standing alliance. He certainly felt that any North Atlantic Treaty should be restricted in purpose to a simple American security guarantee and restricted in geography to states that actually bordered the North Atlantic. Extending it to such decidedly un-Atlantic countries as Italy, Greece and Turkey risked appearing 'to the Soviet leaders as an aggressive encirclement of their country'.[26] Turning it into a standing military organisation risked militarising the confrontation and thereby pushing it onto a plane that favoured the Soviets. Moreover, manning and arming a central European front was going to create a permanent division of Europe, while insisting on a NATO-allied West Germany would foreclose the option of negotiating towards a unified and neutral Germany, thus preventing a broader European settlement as well.

Though not driven by the same anti-New Deal ideology as Taft's conservatism, Kennan, like Taft, also worried that a quasi-imperial role would strain the American economy and dangerously distort the US body politic. Kennan was also concerned that Western Europe's strategic dependency on American protection would sap the Europeans' resolve and capacity to manage their own affairs. In this anxiety, he would later write, 'I was a Gaullist before de Gaulle',[27] and it is indeed instructive to compare the two men's ideas about the symbiosis between American and European power.[28]

Charles de Gaulle's essential view was that America had more power than was good for it or good for the world, more than it sometimes understood and yet less than it often imagined. Such subtleties were not *always* lost on his American interlocutors – along with Kennan, Henry Kissinger was another US official who professed to appreciate and admire de Gaulle's philosophy of power, even if its expression was gratuitously 'wounding' to American sensibilities.[29] Of course, de Gaulle challenged America's power and global leadership during the 1960s, when its limits were becoming painfully obvious to everyone. Four decades later, French President Jacques Chirac criticised American pretensions to unipolar omnipotence at a time when Washington groupthink was fairly well sealed against the possibility that the United States was heading for a fall. Chirac's bad faith was simply assumed, just as de Gaulle's supposedly 'anti-American' animus proved convenient for discounting his warnings about Vietnam. Yet, given that Chirac's warnings on Iraq, like de Gaulle's on Vietnam, turned out to be not just prescient, but also objectively in the service of US interests, it is worth looking back to their roots in a general's vision.

The Gaullist challenge was confounding to American pretensions, not least because it too was an essentially conservative rebuke at a time when the United States was waging cold war on a left–right axis. Such ideological distinctions did not always have strategic salience: America was pretty successful in promoting and aligning with European leftists in the form of anti-communist social democrats who, as often as not, were likely to castigate Washington for taking an insufficiently hard line against Soviet encroachments and intimidation.[30] Still, it looked like a genuine left–right ideological struggle in much of Africa, Asia and Latin America, where post-colonial, nationalist resistance to American hegemony and the American model of modernisation was either explicitly aligned with Soviet interests or susceptible to Maoist, Trotskyite or Castro-style ideologies to a degree that led Washington to discount any supposed independence from Moscow. Washington's embrace of a wide array of right-wing thugs and dictators was one unfortunate consequence of this discounting. In any event, the Americans could be forgiven for assuming that they had their right flank covered.

Yet, in de Gaulle there was a coherent conservative critique of American power and hegemony. The Gaullist critique was not, moreover, *sui generis*: it echoed the conservative anxieties of de Gaulle's American contemporaries such as Kennan and Taft. De Gaulle, naturally, was not as much preoccupied as these Americans with the American domestic political and constitutional damage that they feared would result from an American imperial mission. But like Kennan, he favoured a multi-polar balance of power – a system, in David P. Calleo's words, akin to 'continental Europe's post-Napoleonic balance' instead of recreating 'the worldwide *Pax Brittanica* that enchanted so many American analysts.'[31] Like Kennan, de Gaulle was both appalled by the prospect of a world divided into Soviet and American spheres, and reasonably confident that the enduring force of fissiparous nationalism would render those blocs unsustainable. As president of France, the general did what he could to make the American bloc less manageable.

De Gaulle's at times adversarial relationship with the United States had a lasting impact and American frustration with the Gaullist challenge reached crisis dimensions some three decades later with the transatlantic argument over the Bush administration's decision to invade Iraq. Three months after the start of that campaign, convinced – prematurely – of vindication, the administration set out one of its most elaborate critiques of the Gaullist idea in a speech by National Security Adviser Condoleezza Rice at the London headquarters of the International Institute for Strategic Studies. French concepts of multi-polarity were not only misguided, Rice insisted, but profoundly dangerous:

> Some have spoken admiringly – almost nostalgically – of 'multi-polarity', as if it were a good thing, to be desired for its own sake. The reality is that 'multi-polarity' was never a unifying idea, or a vision. It was a necessary evil that sustained the absence of war but it did not promote the triumph

of peace. Multi-polarity is a theory of rivalry; of competing interests – and at its worst – competing values. We have tried this before. It led to the Great War – which cascaded into the Good War, which gave way to the Cold War. Today this theory of rivalry threatens to divert us from meeting the great tasks before us. Why would anyone who shares the values of freedom seek to put a check on those values? Democratic institutions themselves are a check on the excesses of power. Why should we seek to divide our capacities for good, when they can be so much more effective united? Only the enemies of freedom would cheer this division.[32]

Rice's statement expressed a radical idealism, as recognised by writers such as Calleo and William Pfaff, who have long argued that American power, however benign it might appear, needed to be restrained, which is to say, balanced or contained by a friendly or even opposing force. ('Unwittingly, no doubt,' Calleo wrote after Rice's speech: 'this is the language and mindset of tyranny.')[33] Yet it was at the same time a cogent expression of an enduring American assumption. With important exceptions such as Kennan and Kissinger, Americans have traditionally opposed 'balance-of-power' diplomacy as something anachronistically and even wickedly European. Another way of putting it is that American leaders have generally lacked any notion of power itself as possessing an independent moral dimension. Power has been seen as good or bad depending only on whether good or bad people or states wielded it.

De Gaulle, like Kennan, took a more classically tragic view. Balance of power was a moral imperative in itself, because the possessor of excessive power almost inevitably falls victim to hubris, losing touch with the reality of limits. Such was the downfall of dictators, de Gaulle wrote, it being 'the destiny of all dictators to go too far in what they undertake'.[34] It was the same for unbridled nations. Hence, recalling the Second World War, his famous account of the

> messianic impulse [that] now swelled the American spirit and oriented it toward vast undertakings. The United States, delighting in her resources, feeling that she no longer had in herself sufficient scope for her energies, wishing to help those who were in misery or bondage the world over, yielded in her turn to that taste for interventions in which the instinct for domination cloaked itself.[35]

De Gaulle truly believed that his warnings to US leaders about the hubris of power were friendly warnings.[36] He privately told John F. Kennedy in 1961 that America was repeating France's mistake in Vietnam, and he issued the same warning publicly in 1964. By this time, however, Americans were starting to realise that their house was on fire, and they were highly allergic to any suggestion that it might be, even partly, their own fault.

Cycles of ambition

De Gaulle and Kennan were, in the categories of this book, pluralists. Their warnings about the dangers of imperial over-extension did not bear up perfectly as predictions, something Kennan himself would later admit: contrary to his early fears, the Western allies' position in Berlin turned out to be defensible; US troops in West Germany, though massively present through most of the remaining century, were more welcomed than resented. Still, Kennan and de Gaulle both proved prescient as the Vietnam war turned into a quagmire. The Vietnam disaster was the prelude to the first cycle of managed retrenchment under President Richard Nixon, with the conceptual tutelage of Henry Kissinger. The 'Nixon Doctrine' gave notice that communist insurgencies in other Third World nations would have to be battled by those nations themselves. The United States might give aid, but it would not supply ground forces. In the future, Nixon announced, US interests 'must shape our commitments, rather than the other way around'.[37] Part of the retrenchment involved a phased withdrawal from Vietnam, though of course the war continued another four excruciating years without any better result. Detente with the Soviets relaxed tensions, but was attacked from the right as a strategy born of weakness. Nixon's political self-destruction in Watergate, meanwhile, hardly helped to burnish US credibility.

This cycle of managed retrenchment was reversed, in any event, by two developments. One was the demise of the Soviet Union: whatever credit one chooses to give to more assertive US policies early in the administration of Ronald Reagan, the peaceful conclusion of the Cold War certainly fed into American triumphalism and convictions that the United States was 'the indispensable nation'. The other, earlier development – more fateful than it may have appeared at the time – was the Carter administration's response to the Iranian revolution and the Soviet invasion of Afghanistan. In his 1980 State of the Union Address, President Jimmy Carter declared that 'an attempt by any outside force to gain control of the Persian Gulf region will be regarded as an assault on the vital interests of the United States of America, and such an assault will be repelled by any means necessary, including military force.' This 'Carter Doctrine' laid the conceptual basis for an American strategic engagement that has encompassed two wars against Iraq, another war in Afghanistan, and a build-up of strategic assets that may yet be used in a war with Iran. In Carter's time, of course, the idea of 150,000 troops in any Middle Eastern state would have seemed preposterous. Yet the gradual increase of American deployments followed in the course of 30 years after Carter administration's creation of the Rapid Deployment Joint Task Force, which became Central Command (Centcom).[38]

Under Carter, there also began an American emotional engagement in the Middle East that developed into a difficult entanglement. Americans' moral and emotional ties with Israel were long-standing, though it was only after Carter's stubborn brokering of a peace agreement between Israel and Egypt that those countries came to so dominate the American foreign-aid budget. A darker engagement was the enduring grudge match that developed between the United States and revolutionary Iran following the storming of the US embassy in Tehran in 1979. The ensuing 444-day hostage crisis implanted the image of Iranian brutality deep into the American national psyche. (Similar dark images were planted in the Iranian psyche by American support during Reagan's administration for Iraqi dictator Saddam Hussein's war against Iran, with Washington's merely perfunctory protest against Iraq's strategically significant use of banned chemical weapons.)

The psychological damage of the Iran hostage crisis was not the only legacy to survive Carter's replacement by Reagan. Carter's elevation of human rights as an important portfolio of foreign policy was carried forward by Reagan as well. It is true that, compared to Carter, Reagan's human-rights rhetoric was directed more selectively against communist abuses, but after Carter and Reagan, the idea that championing human rights around the globe was a central purpose of American power now became firmly lodged in the political discourse and the foreign-policy bureaucracy. Reagan also extended the defence-spending increases that Carter initiated after the Soviet invasion of Afghanistan – and, of course, Reagan expanded Carter's programme of military aid for the anti-Soviet mujahadeen. Crucially, the 'supply-side' theory, under which reduced marginal tax rates would generate so much economic growth as to increase tax revenues, had the effect of permanently detaching Republican fiscal policy from Republican defence policy. In the world of real arithmetic, the supply-side theory was refuted almost immediately, as increased defence spending and decreased tax revenue produced large structural fiscal deficits.[39] However, the Keynesian effects of Reagan's deficits, following Federal Reserve Board Chairman Paul Volker's tight monetary policy to squeeze inflation out of the system, contributed to a reasonably robust recovery from the recession of 1980–82: therefore, as Vice President Dick Cheney would later observe, deficits lacked political salience.[40]

With this recovery came the end of the Cold War. Much myth-making has been dedicated to the proposition that Reagan's moral clarity, military aid to Nicaraguan Contras and Afghan mujahadeen, defence build-up and 'Star Wars' ambitions for ballistic-missile defence were the decisive factors convincing the Soviet leadership to undertake radical reform at home and a campaign of diplomatic appeasement abroad. This is a correlation that should not be carelessly confused with causation; in any event, the more obvious correlation was the death by old age of three Soviet party general secretaries in as many years. The younger Mikhail Gorbachev came to power with reformist ambitions that he had nurtured since the Khrushchev thaw (a partial and short-lived relaxation of repression that followed the death of Stalin) of a quarter century earlier.[41] It is arguable, to be sure, that Reagan's rhetoric, together with the evident will and capability of the United States to sustain an protracted arms race, reinforced the framework of containment in which Gorbachev and other Soviet leaders made their crucial choices. Certainly the Soviet decision to liquidate an unwinnable war in Afghanistan was important. Just as certainly, Reagan's personal readiness to trust Gorbachev's sincerity and to engage in some radical diplomatic departures – such as when the two men discussed the abolition of nuclear weapons – provided important reassurance that made Gorbachev more ready and able to settle the Cold War.

Gorbachev's contribution to that settlement was paramount, notably his December 1988 promise, in a speech before the UN General Assembly, to withdraw six tank divisions from Central Europe, and Soviet non-interference the following year when Hungary allowed vacationing East Germans to travel west across the Austrian border. Gorbachev made these decisions under conditions that were partly set by America's four-decades-long strategy of containment. More intriguing than the question of Reagan's particular contribution is the question of whether Kennan's pluralist and less militarised version of the strategy would have yielded the same results – perhaps even years sooner, as Kennan himself argued – compared to the heavily militarised version promoted by Acheson and continued into the Reagan administration.

This counter-factual question may need to wait for a historiography less encumbered by current polemics. What is clear enough today is that the actual American project of Cold War containment produced a military superpower whose strategic hegemony, following the Soviet collapse, was unprecedented. The American superpower proved capable of stupendous feats of power projection, as when the George H.W. Bush administration, leading a broad coalition of forces, was able to drive Iraqi troops out of Kuwait with a one-month air assault and mere 100-hour ground campaign. The now unrivalled superpower proved willing, as well, to fill strategic vacuums, such as when the Clinton administration – having watched while the major European states seemed helpless – finally weighed in with air power and coercive diplomacy to end carnage and genocide in Bosnia and Kosovo.

In both the Persian Gulf and the Balkans, the United States could plausibly be seen to be acting on behalf of the norms and purposes of an 'international community', however nebulously that community might be defined. However, there were also indications of strategic overreach. In Europe, the Clinton administration's policy of NATO enlargement saddled the United States with very considerable new strategic commitments – even if the commitments were undertaken mainly because hardly anyone in the US Congress or administration really believed that they would ever have to be honoured.[42] In the Persian Gulf, American strategic commitments were more tangible and more dangerous. Having defeated Iraqi troops in Kuwait, and hobbled the Saddam regime through fiercely enforced no-fly zones and punitive sanctions, the Reagan strategy of balancing Iraq's Ba'athist dictatorship against revolutionary Iran was now decidedly over. In its stead, the Clinton administration spoke of a policy of 'dual containment', a far more ambitious project.[43]

The cost became evident on 11 September 2001. The proper stipulation that nothing can justify such terrorist crimes should not muddle our historical understanding of the structural connection to America's troop deployments in Saudi Arabia, its enforcement of impoverishing sanctions against Iraq, its decades of support for Arab authoritarians and – of arguably lesser but non-negligible importance – its backing for an Israeli state that maintained an effectively permanent occupation regime over Palestinians. This is not to argue that President George W. Bush's claim that they attacked us because they 'hate our freedoms'[44] was entirely unfounded. Certainly, in the mass murders of 11 September, there was a medievalist and – Bush was right to say – evil rage against secular, Western, cosmopolitan society. But al-Qaeda did not attack Switzerland.

America was deeply entangled and exposed in the Middle East, and the al-Qaeda attacks had the perhaps inevitable consequence of drawing her in further. Still, historians may wonder at how the George W. Bush administration seemed to cast away virtually all the ballast of strategic prudence. Dislodging the Taliban was probably the minimum to expect of any American president under the circumstances, though there was somewhat muddled thinking and discourse about the extent to which America should take responsibility for building and protecting a new Afghan state. The more radical departure was the invasion of Iraq. As Francis Fukuyama wrote in 2005:

> Neither American political culture nor any under-lying domestic pressures or constraints have determined the key decisions in American foreign policy since Sept. 11. In the immediate aftermath of the 9/11 attacks, Americans would have allowed President Bush to lead them in any of several directions, and the nation was prepared to accept substantial risks and sacrifices. The Bush admin-istration asked for no sacrifices from the average American, but after the quick fall of the Taliban it rolled the dice in a big way by moving to solve a longstanding problem only tangentially related to the threat from Al Qaeda – Iraq. In the process, it

squandered the overwhelming public mandate it had received after Sept. 11. At the same time, it alienated most of its close allies, many of whom have since engaged in 'soft balancing' against American influence, and stirred up anti-Americanism in the Middle East.[45]

As Iraq spiralled into civil war and the costs of America's project there became more evident, Americans grew weary of it. Bush narrowly won re-election, but his second term was weighed down by the increasingly unpopular war, among other problems. Barack Obama rose to improbably capture the Democratic nomination for president partly on the basis of his early opposition to the war. Campaigning against the Republican John McCain, Obama promised to end the war 'responsibly', and in more general terms he offered a rebalancing – if not a retrenchment – of what he portrayed as an over-extended foreign policy. Obama won the popular vote decisively, and the electoral college by a landslide.[46]

Moments of restraint

One can therefore trace two broad cycles of post-war American foreign policy. In the first, a steady expansion of military power and hegemonic ambitions started roughly with the Truman Doctrine and continued through repeated escalations of the war in Vietnam. This expansive phase was reversed by the Nixon administration, which withdrew (albeit slowly) from Vietnam and promulgated a Nixon Doctrine whereby such costly engagements were to be avoided in the future, sought détente and arms control with the Soviets and a semi-explicit arrangement of anti-Soviet balancing with China. It seems credible that a genuinely cyclical dynamic was driving these policies, because the popular reaction against the quagmire in Vietnam had slowly but surely reached majority proportions, accompanied by a more elite-driven reaction against the National Security State writ large (as in Senator Frank Church's 1975 committee hearings into past CIA abuses). Nixon won re-election easily against the anti-war Democrat, George McGovern. This was partly because Nixon made skillful appeal to a 'silent majority's' anxiety and resentment about an anarchic counter-culture and anti-war movement. (Nor should we forget the president's 'Southern Strategy' of appealing to white voters who were disaffected by both civil-rights advances and urban disorder.)[47] However, Nixon beat McGovern in 1972 also because he succeeded in co-opting the anti-war weariness of the same middle class: by the summer of that year, when McGovern accepted the Democratic presidential nomination with the refrain, 'Come Home America', most American troops had in fact returned from Vietnam to the United States.[48]

The second cycle in this narrative starts with a Carter–Reagan defence build-up, continues past the Cold War with police action against Iraq's invasion of Kuwait, Clinton's Balkan interventions and then the Bush ground wars in the greater Middle East under the banner of a war on terrorism. Obama then comes to power, as Nixon did, at a time of popular war-weariness and economic stress; and like Nixon, he seeks to narrow American commitments while continuing to defend its core interests.

There is a problem, however, with this cyclical explanation. The Nixon retrenchment was short-lived, and it is far from obvious that the Obama effort will be more enduring – indeed, it could be reversed by the 2012 election. Despite the absence of anything like a peer strategic competitor, America's strategic reach under Obama is comparable to the era when the United States faced the Soviet adversary. Its defense budget, in inflation-adjusted terms, is higher than the Cold War average.[49] Thus, although the cycles appear real enough, the end of the first one did very little to arrest the upward trajectory of American power and responsibility, and it is hard to predict the long-term consequences of a similar Obama strategy.

Analytically, it might be more fruitful to observe that most presidents post-Second World War have had important moments of restraint: episodes in which they made the realist determination to recognise the limits of American power and to avoid over-commitment and unintended consequences. Understanding the reasons for success or failure of their realism could offer insight into the prospects for Obama and his successors.

One could start with Truman's successor, Dwight D. Eisenhower. As a Republican war hero, Eisenhower was comparatively immune to McCarthyite accusations of appeasement and fellow travelling with America's communist adversaries. He flew to Korea as president-elect, fulfilling a campaign promise to figure out how to end an increasingly pointless war there. Upon assuming office, Eisenhower accepted armistice terms. Although his Secretary of State John Foster Dulles promulgated a

doctrine of 'Rollback' to replace the too passive containment, there is no evidence that Eisenhower took this
seriously. Whatever the role of American rhetoric and Radio
Free Europe broadcasts in encouraging the Hungarian
Revolution of 1956, the US never seriously considered intervening to help Hungary against the Soviets.
Eisenhower was mainly furious about another invasion, the
ill-conceived Suez plot between France, Israel and the UK.
In response, Washington engineered a run on the pound,
forcing Britain and its co-conspirators into humiliating
retreat. That the Suez fiasco occurred almost concurrently
with the Soviet repression in Hungary handed Moscow an
extremely helpful propaganda alibi, as far as Washington
was concerned. Eisenhower was angry also for a related
reason: like Obama half a century later, he believed that the
United States and the West had a plausible case to make
in the post-colonial Arab world, but the pitch was significantly undermined by the post-colonial shenanigans of
Suez. (Though of course Eisenhower was not so allergic to
covert action: he approved a CIA-backed coup against the
prime minister of Iran in 1953, along with covert actions in
Guatemala, Indonesia and Cuba.)

President Eisenhower's more fundamental conservatism
related to domestic political economy: he was highly attentive to the economic sources of national power, another
theme that Obama would pick up five decades later. Unlike
the rising right wing of his own party, Eisenhower was
content to accept the basic New Deal welfare state handed
down by his Democratic predecessors. Rhetorically, at least,
he expressed more anxiety about the distorting effects of

military mobilisation, most famously in a farewell warning against a growing 'military industrial complex'.[50] After massive rearmament under Truman, defence spending under Eisenhower flattened out and then fell in real terms.[51] Aside from settling the war in Korea, the most important way that the administration constrained defence spending was by not really preparing to fight a conventional war against the Soviets in Central Europe. Yet, at the same time, the United States was now treaty-obligated to defend its allies in Western Europe. Squaring this dilemma was possible because of nuclear weapons, and the Eisenhower administration's doctrine of 'massive retaliation' for their use: an apocalyptic but relatively cheap promise to unleash full-scale nuclear war if Moscow sent its tank divisions west.

Whether this vow was credible became a matter of debate. During his campaign to replace Eisenhower, Senator John F. Kennedy deployed claims of a 'missile gap' favouring the Soviets as

> the shield from behind which they will slowly, but surely advance – through Sputnik diplomacy, limited brushfire wars, indirect non-overt aggression, intimidation and subversion, internal revolution, increased prestige or influence, and the vicious blackmail of our allies. The periphery of the Free World will slowly be nibbled away ... Each such Soviet move will weaken the West; but none will seem sufficiently significant by itself to justify a nuclear war which might destroy us.[52]

The missile gap turned out to be bogus – the real imbalance strongly favoured the United States. Nevertheless,
once in office, the Kennedy administration appeared in
various ways to be more activist and more energetic than its
cautious predecessor, viewing such energy as the necessary
strategic antidote to Soviet encroachment. In theory, at least,
this Kennedy worldview entailed a maximally demanding
definition of US interests and responsibilities. Hence, in
nuclear policy, the administration developed a doctrine of
'flexible response' – envisioning a graduated use of nuclear
weapons in the event of war. The doctrine was meant to
be less apocalyptic, and therefore more credible and more
effective as the basis of deterrence. If fully resourced, it was
also more expensive. In retrospect, moreover, critics have
argued that it reflected the administration's technocratic
hubris, and was a precursor to the Reagan administration's
later flirtation with nuclear 'war-fighting' doctrine.[53] How,
the critics demanded, could Kennedy or Reagan or any president imagine that, amidst the fog of war, nuclear escalation
would be rational and controlled? Such hubris, it has been
argued, was close cousin to the folly of the administration's
'best and brightest' who designed the staircase of America's
gradual escalation in Vietnam.[54]

There was, however, another side of Kennedy, more
cautious and generally wary of military adventurism.
Recent scholarship supports the contention that Kennedy
was determined to avoid an all-out war in Vietnam, and in
fact rejected at least five separate appeals from his military
and strategic advisers for a major deployment of American
troops there. Kennedy had been a junior naval officer and a

minor war hero in the Second World War, during which he had developed an arguably healthy contempt for the senior generals who were calling on him to escalate.[55]

Kennedy's distrust of the generals also played a role in his careful navigation of the Cuban Missile Crisis. He refused to be goaded into an obsession with 'credibility', he was sensitive to Khruschev's fears of humiliation and encirclement, and he was willing in the end to trade away some missiles in Turkey despite some advisers' pleas that this act of 'appeasement' would demoralise American allies. Despite his well-known anxiety about appearing tough enough, JFK instinctively understood the 'security dilemma'.[56] His views on war and peace focused as much on the First World War's chain of mutual miscalculation as on the West's failure to face down Hitler on the eve of the Second World War. His text on the former was Barbara Tuchman's *The Guns of August*, which he insisted should be read by 'every officer in the Army'.[57] He read Tuchman's book as a blueprint for how crises could spin out of control.

How a completed Kennedy presidency might have balanced these instincts for activism and instincts of restraint is hard to say. But after Cuba, JFK delivered, in his American University commencement speech of 10 June 1963, one of history's great humanist statements of mutual restraint and moral imagination: 'For in the final analysis, our most basic common link is that we all inhabit this small planet. We all breathe the same air. We all cherish our children's futures. And we are all mortal.'[58] Five months later, Kennedy was killed. His successor Lyndon B. Johnson, with the counsel of advisers who had been appointed by his predecessor, expanded Vietnam into one of the ranking disasters of American history. But the Johnson administration also carried forth at least part of the worldview expressed by JFK at American University. Robert McNamara, the defense secretary to both presidents, codified the concepts of nuclear sufficiency and mutual vulnerability as the only viable alternative to a destabilising nuclear arms race. Neoconservative critics attacked these concepts in the 1970s as tantamount to nuclear surrender. Their chief targets by this time were in the Nixon administration, including especially Henry Kissinger, whose realist ideas and attitudes were deemed the antithesis to the traditions of American idealism.[59]

Praise for the Nixon administration requires, firstly, acknowledgment of the huge shadow that Nixon's morose and often vindictive personality cast over American politics and society. Together with the polarising politics of Vietnam, that personality drove the United States into the fateful and utterly unnecessary crisis of Watergate, one consequence of which was that Nixon's national security adviser and later secretary of state, Henry Kissinger, took on an outsized role in making and managing foreign policy for much of Nixon's abbreviated second term.

Nixon and Kissinger were hardly pluralists. The administration that treated the democratic election of Salvador Allende in Chile as so utterly antithetical to American interests, that extended the Vietnam War for another four devastating years, and that expanded that war catastrophically into Cambodia, cannot be described as sanguine or relaxed about the consequences of a more plural distribution of global power. On another level, however, both men seemed aware that an increasingly plural distribution of power was inevitable, and they did work successfully to align that trend with American interests. In this regard, their greatest success was the exploitation of Sino-Soviet rivalry, which Kennan identified as 'the greatest measure of containment that could be conceived'.[60] (Kennan was writing about the rivalry itself, rather than any particular US diplomatic approach to it, but he would also later say of Kissinger: 'Henry understands my views better than anyone at [the] State [Department] ever has.')[61]

Another conspicuous Nixon administration success came in the detachment of Egypt from the Soviet orbit, and its realignment with the United States. (It should be emphasised that this realignment was truly locked in a few years later with President Carter's tireless brokering of the Camp David peace accords between Egypt and Israel, just as Carter had presided over the real normalisation of US relations with post-Mao China.) The Nixon role was interesting, not least because it revealed several layers of administration paradoxes. Firstly, Nixon's role was really, in this instance, Kissinger's: the key crisis of the October 1973 Arab–Israeli war took place during a dramatic episode of the Watergate scandal , the so-called Saturday Night Massacre, in which Nixon fired Special Prosecutor Archibald Cox and then accepted the resignations of Attorney General Elliot Richardson and Deputy Attorney General William Ruckleshaus. Nixon was definitely distracted. Secondly, Kissinger's management of the crisis revealed his great internal tension between a conceptual readiness to accept the independence of allies and a practical unwillingness to accept the consequences of that independence. Thus, at the outset of Nixon's first term, Kissinger urged an agreeable president to dissociate himself from the prevailing Kennedy/Johnson prickliness about de Gaulle's behaviour; before even entering the White House, Kissinger had insisted that the United States 'could not expect to perpetuate the accident of Europe's post-war exhaustion into a permanent pattern of international relations'.[62] Yet when Europeans, led by French Foreign Minister Michel Jobert, tried to assert their independence with a somewhat more pro-Arab approach to the October War and its oil-shock aftermath, Kissinger reacted with fury: the European policies, he would later write, demonstrated the 'demoralisation – verging on abdication – of the democracies' and a choice 'among varieties of appeasement'.[63]

This reaction brings us to a most striking paradox, which is that Kissinger's actual view of the conflict was not far from the Europeans'. The US airlift to Israel and general diplomacy in the crisis constituted a further important step in America's ever-tighter alliance with the Israelis. And yet, in his memoirs, Kissinger praises Anwar Sadat's decision to launch the October War as a strategically enlightened act of statesmanship. The idea, as Kissinger related it, was to create a psychological shock that would enable both Israelis and Arabs to make peace. Israelis needed to be shocked out of their military complacency, while the Egyptians needed liberation from their paralysing national humiliation. Sadat, in Kissinger's view, constituted the rare case of a leader who waged war 'to lay the basis for moderation in its aftermath'.[64]

It was also in the Middle East that Ronald Reagan's administration exercised its own instincts of restraint, and indeed formulated a doctrine to codify that restraint. Again, one should not celebrate realist attitudes without acknowledging moral consequences. Fearing the threat from revolutionary Iran, the Reagan administration engaged in a de facto alliance with Saddam Hussein's Iraq.[65] This tacit US–Iraq alliance may have provoked Iran's Revolutionary Guard Corps to instigate the 1983 Hizbullah truck bombing of US Marine Corps and French paratrooper barracks in Beirut, which killed at least 300. In response, President Reagan did something counter-intuitive and, probably, wise – he withdrew the marines from Lebanon. Some critics, including Reagan's Secretary of State George Shultz, have labelled this withdrawal as the original sin of US appeasement of Islamic terrorism.[66] Though Shultz fought it at the time, he lost to the Pentagon and Defense Secretary Caspar Weinberger, who articulated the eponymous doctrine of strict limits on where and why the United States should go to war. Weinberger spoke for military officers burdened by the legacy of a pointless quagmire in Vietnam, which he did not want to see repeated in the Middle East. Ironically, as John Harper has observed, this made Reagan's the 'first (arguably, the only) administration to adopt a clear and coherent position' on avoiding future Vietnams.[67]

After Reagan's presidency, the Weinberger Doctrine was carried forward as the Powell Doctrine. Its strictures were generally observed in the Gulf War: a time-limited police action using overwhelming military force to achieve clear, finite goals, and then to be withdrawn. Powell himself, still chairman of the Joint Chiefs, used these strictures to try to prevent, and then to criticise, Clinton's forays into the Balkans.[68] In fact, the Balkan interventions did not turn out to be the quagmires that Powell feared, though he might well have worried that their success would foster some insidious assumptions about the American responsibility for wars of humanitarian protection.[69] The Clinton administration was at the same time able to achieve a substantial peace dividend of reductions in real defence spending.

Realist restraint was abandoned during the George W. Bush administration – largely in reaction to the shock of 11 September. Powell, having returned to government service as secretary of state, tried to push his doctrine on the new president in a final formulation: the 'Pottery Barn Rule', whereby if you break it you own it. (Though it was journalist Thomas Friedman, not Powell, who actually named the 'rule'. Moreover, it turned out, to the merriment of some commentators, that Pottery Barn, a chain of American furniture stores, has no such rule.) The president, in any event, was not to be dissuaded from invading Iraq.

There was nothing inevitable about the decision to wage war in Iraq in spring 2003 and, indeed, the war was counter-strategic and damaging to American interests. This is not to say, however, that the decision was entirely *sui generis* in the context of post-Second World War and post-Cold War American foreign policy. The 'Realist' war launched by Bush's father to eject Iraqi forces from Kuwait did not, after all, solve the strategic problem posed by Saddam Hussein's cruelty and defiance. And the US military force for that war was not, in fact, entirely removed: a sizeable contingent remained in Saudi Arabia. A reasonable case could be made that, given American commitments and deployments, the war of regime change in Iraq, even if unwise and badly managed at the time, was likely to come eventually. And if this case is at least arguable, then an overarching question remains open: is the prudence of Realist restraint adequate to avoid creeping and unsustainable US global commitments?

CHAPTER TWO

Barack Obama and the limits of superpower

In the final decade of his life, Osama bin Laden pursued a strategy against America that he had learned – or at least thought he had learned – during the demise of the Soviet Union. Bin Laden's formative experience was in organising support – and fighting in at least one battle himself – for the anti-Soviet resistance in Afghanistan. 'We, alongside the mujaheddin, bled Russia for ten years, until it went bankrupt', he later asserted. This was a somewhat limited version of the story – internal contradictions, sharpened by the West's 40-year strategy of containment, and accelerated by Mikhail Gorbachev's determination to dismantle the regime's most oppressive elements, were most important to the collapse of the USSR. The Afghanistan defeat was an indication of the Soviet Union's overstretch, however, and the leader of al-Qaeda on more than one occasion made explicit comparisons to how he planned to bring down the United States. He would repeat the anti-Soviet success by 'bleeding America to the point of bankruptcy'.[1]

This strategy was based on a highly exaggerated view of American weaknesses as the courage, skill and tenacity of America's security forces in hunting him down at least partly indicate. One must concede, however, that he was shrewd about the national psychology that would compel the United States to expend vast treasure and blood in reaction to the attacks of 11 September 2001. The financial costs of the Iraq War and the Afghanistan War, together with upgrades to general counter-terrorism and homeland security, amount to trillions over the past decade.[2] There arguably were also huge indirect costs stemming, as Ezra Klein has written, from the Federal Reserve's decision to cut interest rates to counter both a possible 'fear-induced recession' as well as high oil prices after the Iraq invasion. 'That decade of loose monetary policy may well have contributed to the credit bubble that crashed the economy in 2007 and 2008.'[3] These are economic costs. The American reaction to 11 September also destroyed or blighted hundreds of thousands of lives in Iraq and Afghanistan and degraded America's moral reputation at Abu Ghraib and Guantanamo. In broader strategic terms, the United States was weakened by being drawn into land wars in the Middle East and South-Central Asia.[4]

The Saudi terrorist had made 'a smart play against a superpower', as Klein observed in reflecting on bin Laden's death. 'We didn't need to respond to 9/11 by trying to reshape the entire Middle East, but we're a superpower, and we think on that scale. We didn't need to respond to failed attempts to smuggle bombs onto airplanes through shoes and shampoo bottles, but we're a superpower, and our tolerance for risk is extremely low.'[5] Regardless of whether he consciously intended or understood it at the time, Osama bin Laden effectively laid a trap that America would walk into.

Assuming office, President Barack Obama appeared to be aware of this trap, and determined to get out of it. Step one was to get out of Iraq. In making good on his campaign promise to do so, Obama was helped by the relative success of President Bush's 2006 'surge' of US forces there, as well as the 2008 Status of Forces Agreement that the Bush administration had concluded with Iraq's government. The politics of both were complicated. Then Senator Obama, along with much of the US foreign-policy establishment, had opposed the surge as a futile prolongation of an unwinnable war. In truth, the calming of Iraq's civil war happened thanks to a broad array of enabling factors, including the revulsion of Sunni tribal leaders in Anbar province at the savage behaviour of their al-Qaeda allies, and their recruitment by US military commanders, through money payments and other blandishments, to switch sides. However, the new strategy implemented by General David Petraeus, focused on protecting civilians as much or more than killing insurgents, was also important, and that strategy benefitted from Bush's deployment of additional troops.

The Status of Forces Agreement (SOFA) set a deadline of 2012 for the complete withdrawal of US forces. While agreed by Bush, it was pushed by the government of Nuri al-Maliki, which was partly emboldened by Obama's campaign rhetoric, as well as the strong desire of many Iraqis to see the back of US forces. Obama, as president, was resolute in sticking to the timetable in spite of re-erupting violence, and he seemed relatively relaxed about Baghdad's refusal to negotiate a new

SOFA that would have allowed a residual US force to operate with immunity to Iraqi law. Although Republicans fiercely criticised the failure to negotiate a continued military presence, public opinion sided with the president. That Americans, by a clear majority, wanted completely out of Iraq said something about the future appetite for such deployments.[6]

Afghanistan

Obama's more difficult inheritance was the war in Afghanistan. His administration's struggle to deal with this constitutes an important case study in the tensions at the heart of Obama's national-security strategy, so it is worth examining it at some length. In Afghanistan, Democratic president was, in certain respects, hoist by his and his party's own political petard. Democrats for generations have struggled against voters' judgements that they are not as tough as Republicans when it comes to confronting America's enemies. In criticising George W. Bush's foreign policy in general, and the Iraq War in particular, the Democratic politicians took great and repeated pains to emphasise that they were not pacifists. Obama was an Illinois state senator when he opened his speech to a 2002 anti-Iraq war rally in Chicago with the declaration: 'I don't oppose all wars ... What I am opposed to is a dumb war.'[7] It became a standard Democratic argument that one of the big problems with President Bush's rush to war in Iraq was that it caused the administration to neglect the more important and more justified war in Afghanistan. It was not, after all, from Iraq, but from Afghanistan, that the 11 September attacks were planned and directed.[8]

In his 2004 campaign to unseat President Bush, Senator John Kerry hit out frequently at the frustrating and embarrassing battle of Tora Bora three years earlier, when American commanders were convinced they were close to capturing or killing Osama bin Laden, only to have him slip away through the mountains into Pakistan. Kerry claimed that preoccupation with and preparations for Iraq meant there had been inadequate force levels in Afghanistan, including Tora Bora, where the US instead had to rely on anti-Taliban Afghans under the banner of the Northern Alliance.[9] Obama carried the same argument into the 2008 presidential campaign.[10] Such arguments expressed a recognisable liberal internationalist perspective that was based as much on moral reasoning as strategic logic. The United States was deemed to have 'abandoned' Afghanistan as the fall of the Soviet-backed regime there gave way to a devastating, decade-long civil war. Having returned to Afghanistan after 11 September, it seemed incumbent upon the United States and its allies to do things right this time – above all, not to let the country again fall victim to the medieval cruelties of Taliban rule.

Such liberal interventionism had been tested in the Balkan interventions of the Clinton administration, and was a topic of debate in the 2000 presidential campaign. Republican candidate George W. Bush and his advisers argued that the United States should not squander finite strategic resources on quixotic projects of nation-building. 'We don't need to have the 82nd Airborne escorting kids to kindergarten', was Bush adviser Condeleezza Rice's memorable way of arguing that US troops should not be tied down in lengthy Balkans missions.[11] Then Vice President Al Gore, the Democratic candidate, responded with a full-throated defence of what the United States and its European allies had accomplished with military interventions and extended peacekeeping missions in Bosnia and Kosovo.[12] Bush won the election but the Democrats arguably won that particular argument, insofar as the new Republican administration decided against a precipitous withdrawal of American troops from the Balkans, on the grounds that it would be too unsettling to alliance relationships.

In its military responses to 11 September, however, the administration did continue to exhibit an allergic attitude towards heavy commitments of infantry forces to what it deemed to be unnecessary projects of social engineering. The initial war in Afghanistan was not so much a US invasion as the application of air power and special forces to tip the balance towards one side, the Northern Alliance, in Afghanistan's ongoing civil war. (Even many years later, Bush's second defense secretary, Robert Gates, expressed his concerns that a larger military footprint might repeat the Soviet Union's failed campaign to pacify the country.)[13] For the invasion of Iraq, civilians and officers in Donald Rumsfeld's Pentagon were beguiled by a misleading view of what 'transformational' technologies could accomplish with a relatively small number of troops.[14]

In both cases, arguably, but certainly in Iraq, the United States suffered real debacles borne in part of an egregious mismatch between war aims and invested resources. The Democratic critique of this mismatch was largely correct, and it was elaborated in detailed work by a RAND Corporation team under veteran diplomat James Dobbins, an accomplished Balkans and Afghanistan hand, who observed that when it comes to nation-building, there is a direct relationship between input (in terms of troop numbers and other resources) and output (in successful peace, stability and development).[15] These RAND studies helped establish as a rule of thumb that successful nation-building projects required one soldier or police officer for every 40 to 50 members of the population being protected.

By the time of George W. Bush's second term, however, the partisan line-up on the question of a large versus small military footprint for nation-building had been jumbled. In part this was because the main justification for invading Iraq – Saddam Hussein's nuclear, biological and chemical weapons programmes – turned out to be groundless. By default, President Bush turned to his other, grander rationale – using American military power to spread democracy in the Middle East. This had always been part of the package, but it seemed increasingly ridiculous as Iraq descended into a savage sectarian war. What saved the rationale, at least in Republican eyes, was the success of the 'surge' of American forces in Iraq which, after 2006, seemed to turn around a losing war. President Bush and his dwindling supporters felt vindicated, and Senator John McCain, the 2008 Republican candidate for president, used the surge's apparent success to argue that Obama, who had opposed it, lacked the judgement to command America's military establishment.

Besides partisan politics, there were military politics. General Petraeus was the most visible of a group of dissident officers who challenged what they regarded as the Pentagon's faddish fixation on an information-technology driven 'Revolution in Military Affairs'. This fixation had, in the view of the dissidents, left America unprepared for real wars in urban settings such as Iraq, where no amount of computer-networked 'information dominance' could compensate for the American army's essential ignorance about the language, culture, motivations and politics of insurgencies it was trying to suppress and the nation it was trying to build and sustain. As then-Colonel H.R. McMaster, an intellectual allied with Petraeus, argued in *Survival*:

> thinking about defence was driven by a fantasti-
> cal theory about the character of future war rather
> than by clear visions of emerging threats to national
> security in the context of history and contempo-
> rary conflict. Proponents of what became known
> as military transformation argued for a 'capabili-
> ties based' method of thinking about future war.
> In practice, however, capabilities-based analysis
> focused narrowly on how the United States would
> *like* to fight and then assumed that the preference
> was relevant.[16]

According to McMaster, 'self-delusion about the character of future conflict [had] weakened US efforts in Afghanistan and Iraq as war plans and decisions based on flawed visions of war confronted reality.' This included the reality that Iraq and Afghanistan were wars of counter-insurgency that required winning the support of the local peoples who constituted the main stake in the struggle. This meant living among them, rather than barrelling past or over them in intimidating armoured vehicles, and convincing them that the Americans were not occupiers but rather protectors. This, in turn, required large numbers of well-trained troops.

Without quite saying he had been wrong about the Iraq surge, the new President Obama made clear that he wanted to learn from its successes and apply them to Afghanistan. Yet, in the series of Afghan strategy reviews that he commissioned in the first year of his administration, a rather awkward question emerged. Though no one would have put it quite this way, the question was essentially this: what if the Bush administration had it right the first time?

The point of the question is not to challenge the now-conventional wisdom that the Bush administration neglected Afghanistan and woefully mishandled Iraq. Yet it is arguable that the Bush administration's initial instinct of avoiding an ambitiously defined Afghanistan mission was the right one. The case would go something like this: the United States had suffered a devastating attack for which the Taliban regime, as al-Qaeda's host, was partly responsible. But Mullah Omar, the Taliban leader, probably did not know about the 11 September attacks before they happened, and Washington's initial response came in the form of an ultimatum: hand over bin Laden and other key al-Qaeda leaders, or wait for the destruction of your regime. Implicit in this ultimatum was the possibility that Mullah Omar and the Taliban would comply, and that the United States and its allies would then have left the Taliban and Afghan people to their own devices. Admittedly, the scenario was never very probable. But, had it transpired, would it have been reasonable to argue that the United

States had failed to respond adequately to the 11 September attacks?

The argument, in other words, is that strategic-level acts of terrorism may indeed require a strategic-level response: in effect, regimicide.[17] But to go even further, by attempting to re-engineer a society and a nation of almost 30 million people, the US risked strategic over-stretch on a tragic scale, thereby falling into the terrorist's classical trap. Arguably, the US should have helped destroy the Taliban, and then left.

This is not to suggest that the Bush administration pursued anything resembling such a narrowly defined strategy. On the contrary, under Bush an incoherent and under-resourced Afghanistan war drifted for seven years.[18] The US was joined in this drift by NATO allies, and for much of that time Afghanistan was argued about as a test of alliance solidarity without any clear or common understanding of what the alliance was trying to achieve there, or whether it was achievable. Likewise, Obama came into office promising to do a better job – without, however, having undertaken a rigorous examination of what that job actually was or should be. To his credit, having responded in his first months in office to what his military officers said was a general deterioration on the ground with an order to reinforce troop levels with another 17,000 soldiers, he insisted that before the *next* escalation there would be such an assessment.

That policy review took place over a period of months during autumn 2009, and created, inside the administration, the most intense foreign-policy argument of Obama's first term, an argument that the *Washington Post's* Bob

Woodward narrated in his book *Obama's Wars*.[19] One faction included Petraeus, who was then CENTCOM commander, the Chairman of the Joint Chiefs Admiral Mullen, and the newly appointed commander in Afghanistan, General Stanley McChrystal. These officers used the Iraq experience to push for a fully manned counter-insurgency campaigned aimed at winning over the Afghan population and reversing the Taliban's momentum. McChrystal immediately upon his appointment toured Afghanistan and drafted a lengthy and dire assessment of a war that was on the verge of being lost. (Somebody leaked the classified assessment to Woodward, who published it in the *Washington Post*, to the consternation of the White House.) Without another 40,000 troops, McChrystal concluded, the US and its allies faced 'mission failure'.[20]

The contending faction, led by Vice President Joe Biden, and including many of Obama's top political advisers, considered any Afghan escalation to be unavoidably under the shadow of Vietnam, strategically incoherent and disconnected from any overriding American interest or purpose. The United States had been drawn into Afghanistan by al-Qaeda's attack on the United States, but al-Qaeda in the meantime had been driven mainly out of Afghanistan and into Pakistan, where its leadership enjoyed de facto sanctuary. Nothing that the US could do in Afghanistan would change the reality that the military and especially intelligence leadership of a precarious Pakistan was playing a double game: fighting with considerable heroism and sacrifice against Islamist militants in tribal areas, yet at the same time hedging with continued support for the very Taliban that it had helped create in the first place. How to change Pakistan's behaviour was an excruciating problem, but banging America's head against the door in Afghanistan could do little to solve that problem.

The nightmare scenarios for American interests included a takeover of the Pakistani state and its nuclear weapons by the Islamist militants that Pakistan had nurtured as weapons against India, or an Indo-Pakistani nuclear war. Indeed, it was feared that the former could actually lead to the latter. Pakistan's schizoid behaviour was said to stem from its fear of being isolated and surrounded by a huge and conventionally superior India. But Obama himself, according to Woodward's account, noted the contradiction in arguing that America had to stay in Afghanistan to reassure Pakistan against another strategic abandonment, since the ostensible American *purpose* in Afghanistan was to strengthen the government of Hamid Karzai, which Pakistan considered an Indian puppet, and as such was determined to undermine. Strengthening the Karzai government was a losing proposition in any event, according to the Biden faction. The Kabul regime's intractable corruption and mal-governance was a primary and renewable source of Taliban strength.

Against the generals, Biden and his allies argued strenuously for a more limited strategy that they dubbed 'counterterrorism plus'. In essence, it was a strategy for maintaining major American military bases and supporting the Kabul government in those places where its writ plausibly ran, but not attempting to pacify all of Afghanistan or train a massive 400,000-man army. Instead, the Americans would train a more realistically sized force and otherwise focus on destroying terrorists, both those few remaining in Afghanistan and the more numerous in Pakistan. Negotiations and some sort of power sharing with the more reconcilable elements of the Taliban would be encouraged. Among other virtues, this was seen to be a strategy that could be replicated in other places where al-Qaeda had established itself, including Somalia and Yemen (whereas it was unthinkable that the US would repeat its Afghan counter-insurgency and nation-building efforts).

The Vietnam analogy can be a careless cliché. But the problem of civil–military tensions that constrained Obama's decision-making did have an instructive precedent in the early 1960s. Chapter one has discussed how President Kennedy refused to be cowed by – and indeed, showed some disdain for – senior military commanders. In contrast to JFK, Obama lacked the prestige-enhancing background of military service, but he did try to avoid being boxed in by the military. It was not easy. The president and his political advisers became intensely frustrated by the Pentagon's refusal to present him with realistic options other than the generals' preferred package of 40,000 new troops. They were also concerned that military commanders were using their connections in the press and the Republican Party to pre-empt the conclusions of the policy review. This concern came to a head in October 2009 when General McChrystal delivered a speech at the London headquarters of the IISS. Asked in general terms about Biden's preferred counter-terrorism strategy, McChrystal called it 'short-sighted' and said it would lead to 'Chaos-istan'.[21] According to Woodward's account, 'McChrystal's comments marked a seminal moment for the White House staff. What better proof that the military was on a search-and-destroy mission aimed at the president?'[22]

For policy reasons Obama did, of course, need to take military advice seriously, and for political reasons he could not afford an open break with his commanders. The die was probably cast when both Defense Secretary Gates and Secretary of State Hillary Clinton came down in support of the more ambitious strategy. More generally, the decision was constrained by a form of status quo bias: however fallacious it might be to argue on the basis of already sunk costs, it was difficult to abandon an eight-year military effort without investing in one more try.

In the end, the president approved another 30,000 troops, most of what the military had asked for. But he also tried to establish his own authority and a more narrowly defined mission through a six-page, single-spaced 'terms sheet' that he dictated himself. The intent would be to 'degrade', rather than defeat or destroy, the Taliban. There would be no country-wide counter-insurgency effort, Obama insisted, and there would be no unrealistic commitment to train a massive army of 400,000 Afghan troops. The mission was to be limited in geography and time. By July 2011, the terms sheet stated, 'we will expect to begin transferring lead security responsibility from these [US] forces to the [Afghan] ANSF and begin reducing U.S. forces to the levels below the extended surge.'[23]

It was a nuanced outcome, starting with ambiguity about what the July 2011 date actually meant, and it opened the president to criticism from all sides. Supporters of the war complained that any deadline, however soft, would embolden the enemy to simply wait for America and its allies to leave.[24] War sceptics feared the date was too elastic to set any serious limit on the American commitment; moreover, since they suspected the president of sharing their scepticism, they accused him of squandering more money and more lives on a hopeless cause.[25] The president's terms sheet stated that the 'total cost for this option in Afghanistan is about US$113 billion per year for those years in which we sustain nearly 100,000 troops in Afghanistan.'[26] For how many more years, the sceptics asked, could Washington justify spending more than $100bn on this war?

Within 19 months, the president clarified his own answer to this question. On 21 July 2011, Obama announced that 33,000 troops would be withdrawn from Afghanistan by September 2012, with 10,000 leaving before the end of 2011. This was at the accelerated end of the options he had been presented, and both Secretary Gates, who was about to retire, and Afghan commander Petraeus, who was about to take over as director of the CIA, had argued for a slower drawdown. But Obama's decision seemed consonant with a rough public and elite consensus. A complete withdrawal is not on the cards for the foreseeable future, but America's relationship with Afghanistan after 2016 – whatever happens on the battlefield and regardless of whether Taliban fighters can be induced to trade weapons for power sharing – is likely to consist of aid, military training, and one or two bases from which American soldiers can support the Afghan government and American special forces can continue to target and kill al-Qaeda-linked terrorists. 'This is neither counter-insurgency nor nation-building. The costs are prohibitive', is how Obama put it in 2009, according to Bob Woodward; it is hard to imagine the circumstances under which he would change that position.[27]

Republican critics accused the president of telegraphing a lack of will to the Taliban, inviting the insurgents, in effect, to wait America out. The accusation is fair, but the alternative is not so clear. And it cannot be assumed that a Republican president inaugurated in 2013 or 2017 would set a fundamentally different course. It is, in any event, almost impossible for a large, transparent democracy such as the United States to effectively bluff about commitments and goals that go – as Obama put it at West Point – 'beyond our responsibility, our means, or our interests'.

America: offshore balancer?

By early 2012, the Obama administration had both reaffirmed its deadline for substantial withdrawal from Afghanistan, and released a defence budget planning document that envisioned substantial overall reductions in US infantry forces. At roughly the same time, a largely symbolic deployment of US marines to Australia underscored the idea of a strategic pivot towards the Asia-Pacific, where a careful balancing of China's rise could, it was hoped, be accomplished without provoking a destructive arms race. Much of the pivot was diplomatic; US officials argued that Washington's renewed attention to Asia-Pacific allies had already bolstered their confidence and restored a psychological balance vis-à-vis Beijing.[28] Meanwhile, against al-Qaeda, the new administration moved aggressively to ramp up the intelligence war, of which the most tangible products were drone operations in Pakistan, Afghanistan and Yemen. Though probably legal under the UN mandate that followed 11 September,[29] these targeted killings inevitably caused collateral civilian deaths and a great deal of anger with the United States. Public outrage was particularly manifest in Pakistan, where opinion polling unsurprisingly shows that consistent majorities are offended by the drone strikes.[30] Yet, against this contribution to the moral deficit, the administration could be reasonably satisfied that it was keeping al-Qaeda's leadership on the run, its command-and-control degraded, and its capability to attack the United States limited. Most dramatically, of course, the intelligence war included an uncertain and perilous operation that succeeded in killing Osama bin Laden.

President Obama's decision to launch the operation on 2 May 2011 was a risky one: there was only indirect evidence that bin Laden was actually in the Abbottabad compound; if the mission had failed, with American deaths and Pakistani victims, Barack Obama would have been pilloried as relentlessly as Jimmy Carter after an analogous failure 31 years before.[31] But the mission did not fail. Its success, a triumph for US intelligence and special forces, as well as an undoubted political win for the American president, also fitted well with an emerging Obama doctrine of muscular but more narrowly focused pursuit of American interests. This doctrine follows a recognisable template. Peter Beinart wrote:

> There's a name for the strategy the Obama admin-
> istration is increasingly pursuing from the Persian

Gulf to the South China Sea: offshore balancing. It's the idea that America can best contain our adversaries not by confronting them on land, but by maintaining our naval and air power and strengthening those smaller nations that see us as a natural counterweight to their larger neighbors.[32]

The trouble with such a strategy is that strategic and moral commitments have a way of coming due: offshore balancing can become onshore war. Sunk costs, as in Afghanistan; humanitarian outrage, as in Libya and Syria; proliferation threats, as in Iran and North Korea: these and more have a way of drawing the United States into military engagements that may become land wars. America may choose to build up allies instead of confronting its adversaries directly; it may use air power instead of land forces to contain potential rivals, and yet these strategies may prove unsustainable. Nonetheless, offshore balancing is a reasonable template for what the Obama administration is trying to do, and one that makes sense for an overstretched United States to pursue.

The previous chapter touched on the Nixon Doctrine as an earlier project to ameliorate the problems of American over-extension, in Southeast Asia most acutely. It was a time, as David Calleo has observed, when a 'variety of radical trends ... pointed toward the end of the Cold War and a more plural world to follow'. These included the Sino-Soviet schism and Egypt's disaffection with its Soviet patron. Calleo observes that 'Richard Nixon and Henry Kissinger turned these trends to America's advantage'.[33] If Obama was to find a lasting solution to overstretch, his administration needed to likewise work with the grain of history and turn it to America's advantage.

The first step in this regard was to foster the conditions that would allow a substantial withdrawal from the Greater Middle East, with the ultimate goal of returning to the kind of 'over-the-horizon' posture that prevailed through the Reagan administration.[34] Events in the region arguably served in some ways to advance this goal, but in other ways made it more difficult. The most critical problem for Washington stemmed from its confrontation with Iran. This problem, which posed the biggest obstacle to any strategy of partial withdrawal from the region, is addressed in detail later in this chapter. At the outset of Obama's third year in office, a tumultuous Arab Awakening challenged decades-long American assumptions and relationships. Certain dimensions of this awakening undoubtedly served US interests: foremost, the mass demands for real democracy constituted a decisive repudiation of al-Qaeda's residual claims to lead a pan-Islamic insurgency against global civilisation. More ambiguous and troubling, however, were the potential consequences if democratic demands were thwarted, if economic aspirations could not be met, or if popular revolutions were hijacked by ruthless radicals or fundamentalists.

The United States could not address either Iran's nuclear ambitions or the Arab Awakening without giving serious consideration to its alliance with Israel. Understanding that alliance is essential for understanding the US strategic commitment to the Middle East. The 'Israel lobby' is unquestionably a powerful force in Washington, but fixation on it can obscure the true dimensions of the US–Israel connection. Jewish voters may be important in key states, but they are predominantly liberal and vote mainly Democratic: in the 2008 presidential election, despite energetic Republican efforts to label him an 'appeaser' who would sell Israel down the river, Barack Obama won an estimated 78% of the Jewish vote. But the American constituency for reflexively supporting the Israeli government of the day overlaps only partially with American Jews.

There is a general inclination to see the Jewish state as an embattled democracy reflecting American values, as well as a specific minority of 'Christian Zionists' whose discourse now dominates the Republican Party. Republican presidential candidate Mitt Romney has argued, in so many words, that US policy should not deviate from the preferences of the Israeli government.[35] Former House Speaker Newt Gingrich, while challenging Romney for the nomination in 2012, argued that Palestinians are an 'invented people' who should find someplace other than Palestine to live.[36] If such statements constitute the threshold for being 'pro-Israel', then Obama fails the test.

But the divergence between Washington's and Jerusalem's definitions of their respective national interests predates Obama. The George H.W. Bush administration got into a bitter dispute with the Yitzhak Shamir government over Jewish settlements in occupied territories, while Clinton administration interactions with the first Benjamin Netanyahu government became positively poisonous. Under Obama, the problem arguably grew even more serious. While military ties between the United States and Israel remained robust, political relations between the White House and

Netanyahu's rightist coalition had become fraught. The Israelis were deeply suspicious from the outset of candidate Obama's declared intentions to change the nature of America's relations with the rest of the Middle East.

The US president has insisted all along that America could change its relationship with the Middle East while remaining true to its Israeli ally. At the beginning of his presidency, Obama had launched a kind of moral demarche to the world's Arabs and Muslims. Heralded in his June 2009 speech in Cairo, this démarche had included the overtures to Iran, the repudiation of torture, closing of Guantanamo, and Obama's demand to Israel for a settlements freeze and progress on the peace process.[37] Underlying the speech was a simple premise: America would find it hard to pursue its interests and its values if it had to swim in a sea of Arab hostility. Yet, the Cairo speech became a prime example of the gap between Obama's lofty promises and his limited power. Although torture was duly repudiated, America was denied much of the credit for that repudiation, because Congress refused to grant the symbolic victory of closing Guantanamo. And hopes raised in Cairo were destroyed almost immediately by the intransigence of Israel's coalition government, which refused to stop building settlements in occupied territory and thereby delivered to the president the most dramatic foreign-policy defeat of his first term in office.

By summer 2011, Netanyahu's trips to Washington were becoming occasions of barely disguised animosity between the prime minister and the president. A repeat performance, scheduled around Netanyahu's May 2011 visit to address the annual convention of the American Israel Public Affairs Committee, the most powerful pro-Israel lobbying group in the United States, became even more fraught after Republican House Speaker John Boehner invited Netanyahu also to address a joint session of Congress. Concerned that the Israeli leader would use the occasion to leverage pro-Israeli sentiment against the administration, Obama aides scheduled the president to go first with another major speech on the Middle East. Though framed mainly as an American response to the Arab Awakening, Obama also used the occasion to set out a more explicit American commitment to a two-state solution based on pre-1967 borders with land-swaps to accommodate the largest Jewish settlements. Netanyahu responded with another sharp rejection of the president's vision and policies. The 1967 borders were a complete non-starter, he said before, during and after his meeting in the White House, in his address to AIPAC, and his speech before Congress – which responded with 29 standing ovations.[38]

White House aides were mystified. Though Obama had been somewhat clearer than past presidents, the 1967 parameters were the underlying policy of every administration going back to Lyndon B. Johnson immediately after the June 1967 war. The concept had been embraced by Netanyahu's defence minister, Ehud Barak, when he was Labour prime minister negotiating with Yassir Arafat, and by Netanyahu's immediate predecessor, Ehud Olmert. The current prime minister's shrill rejection of the same parameters could only suggest real doubt about the sincerity of his recent, and palpably grudging, embrace of the two-state concept. Israel's government was alarmed about, yet at the same time seemed oddly oblivious to, the strategic implications of the Arab Awakening. Though the administration was committed to trying to head off a UN resolution recognising a Palestinian state, which the Palestinians planned to introduce in September, Obama also argued that the empowerment of Arab peoples could only make the Israeli occupation even less tenable. Clearly, the Israel–Palestine problem was not the driving cause that had inspired Arab populations to rise up against their rulers. Just as clearly, the arrival of real politics to Arab lands would place new expectations and pressures on Israel and its American ally.

The Arab Awakening had already underlined the sharp limits to Washington's ability to anticipate, much less control, events of seismic importance. This was an old story of an American intelligence community that could plainly see that autocratic regimes wouldn't last forever, but was helpless to predict when the fall might come. A chain of events was set off in late 2010, when Tunisian fruit and vegetable vendor Mohammed Bouazizi, frustrated by the behaviour of officials, set himself on fire. His act brought Tunisians on to the streets in a protest that went on to convulse much of the Arab world. Washington rightly considered Egypt, containing half of the world's Arabs, to be the strategic pivot. Egypt had also been an America ally for more than three decades, during which it had maintained a critical peace treaty with Israel. And for most of those years, Egypt had been touted as Exhibit A by those who argued that the American interest in regional stability entailed excessive moral collusion with despotic regimes.

The decision to help push President Hosni Mubarak out of office thus entailed real dilemmas for US policy – some compared it to President Jimmy Carter's abandonment of the shah of Iran in 1979 – but standing indefinitely behind the Egyptian regime was not a viable option. Obama was predictably criticised for his characteristically hedged response. It was not in his conservative nature to lean very far forward in declaiming for a democratic revolution, and he justified this caution by insisting that real empowerment of the Egyptian people required less rather than more association with American aims. However, the administration warned publicly and in strong terms against violent repression of the demonstrations, while privately employing the two countries' close military-to-military contacts to involve the Egyptian army in ending Mubarak's rule.

In so navigating the crisis, the administration was following some well-worn tracks. By 2011, democracy promotion was the default foreign policy of the United States, and it had wide US support. To be sure, in the early jockeying for the next US election, right-wing presidential aspirants, including Gingrich and Minnesota Congresswoman Michelle Bachman, attacked the president for abandoning an ally and opening the door for an Islamist takeover of Egypt.[39] More broadly, however, the Republican Party's foreign-policy elites – roughly speaking, the neoconservatives – recognised the cognitive dissonance in supporting democracy while fixating on a potential threat from the Muslim Brotherhood. Without precisely saying that the president had done a good job, the neoconservatives broadly supported his Egyptian policy.

Another key American ally, Saudi Arabia, was far less happy about that policy. Uninterested in American lectures about inevitable democratic change, the Saudis added to US difficulties in the region by sending troops across the causeway to support the repression of demonstrations in the adjacent Gulf kingdom of Bahrain. Bahrain was home base to the American Fifth Fleet, a key element in the US plan to contain Iran, and moving the fleet elsewhere in the Gulf was not a real option since no other Gulf Cooperation Council (GCC) state would be keen to offend the Bahrainis, or Saudis, by accepting it. GCC ruling families claimed anyway that containing Iran was very much the point of repressing the Shia protesters in Bahrain who, according to Gulf Arab leaders, were mere tools of Iranian mischief. Washington rejected that diagnosis, and warned that legitimate Shia grievances could indeed be turned into Iranian assets if Bahrain's rulers did not handle them wisely. 'The only way forward', Obama said of Bahrain in his May 2011 speech on the Middle East, 'is for the government and opposition to engage in a dialogue, and you can't have a real dialogue when parts of the peaceful opposition are in jail.' The president pointed in the same speech to Yemen, another key ally where the United States was trying to uproot an al-Qaeda presence; 'President [Ali Abdullah] Saleh', Obama said, 'needs to follow through on his commitment to transfer power.' There were definite limits, however, beyond which the administration would not push. In practice, US policy was devolving into what one Pentagon official called a 'bifurcated' strategy that emphasised stability in the Gulf and democracy in North Africa.[40] This inconsistency reflected the kinds of moral compromises that may be inherent to relying on regional allies.

Humanitarian war

There was, as already noted, reason to wonder whether the Arab Awakening would really push Middle East politics in a direction that would render American commitments and responsibilities less onerous and more manageable. Extremism and violence would weigh on the more onerous side of the ledger. And extremism and violence arrived, with the brutal repressions in Libya and Syria. Muammar Gadhafi's attacks on protesters and the threatened siege of Benghazi in particular led America into a third war in the greater Middle East that the Obama administration had so much wanted to avoid.

Having in 2003 negotiated with the United States and Britain to abandon nuclear- and chemical-weapons programmes, Gadhafi had been supported in a quid pro quo deal for international rehabilitation. That rehabilitation ended abruptly in February 2011, when the Libyan dictatorship fired on its own protesters and then bore down on Benghazi, threatening to hunt the rebels from house to house, 'like rats'. Soon afterwards, mere weeks after the Libyan protests and repression started, the UN Security Council authorised member states to use 'all necessary measures' to keep Gadhafi's forces from the hunt.[41] In the history of a putative international community organising itself to stop atrocities, this was the speed of light and, as Bruce Jones explains, only the fourth time in its history that the Security Council 'fully' authorised 'force against a member state'.[42]

The resolution – its passage enabled by arguably construc- tive abstentions from Russia and China – was surprisingly robust, with language conforming to American prefer- ences. It was preceded, however, by a fierce debate within the administration, one that pitted Secretary of State Hillary Clinton, who favoured an intervention, against Gates, who was far more cautious. Gates worried about being drawn into a long-term conflict with unclear aims.

Clinton won the argument, but for some weeks there was reason to worry that Obama, in league with France's Nicolas Sarkozy and Britain's David Cameron, had thereby stum- bled into his own dumb war. It could be argued, however, that the Obama administration did not have much choice. It was going to be difficult for the United States to stand aside as Gadhafi's troops went from house to house in Benghazi. 'It was not in our national interest to let that happen,' Obama said in his 28 March speech explaining his decision.[43] This was not some post hoc rationalisation; the obligation for humanitarian intervention had been a clear argument of his 2009 Nobel Peace Prize acceptance speech:

> More and more, we all confront difficult questions
> about how to prevent the slaughter of civilians by
> their own government, or to stop a civil war whose
> violence and suffering can engulf an entire region.
> I believe that force can be justified on humanitar-
> ian grounds, as it was in the Balkans, or in other
> places that have been scarred by war. Inaction tears
> at our conscience and can lead to more costly inter-
> vention later. That's why all responsible nations

must embrace the role that militaries with a clear
mandate can play to keep the peace.[44]

The Libya action may not have been the perfect occasion
for humanitarian intervention but there is, in truth, unlikely to
be a better one. The emergency was real and impending. The
response was authorised by the UN Security Council, with
five abstentions but no vetoes or negative votes. Through the
Arab League, regional states supported it. Nearer powers –
France and Britain – argued for it and were willing to take on
the main burden of conducting it. If one believes in the developing international norm of a 'responsibility to protect' – and
according to its vote of 14 September 2009, the UN General
Assembly does so believe – then this particular exercise of
that responsibility is probably as good as it gets.[45]

Obligation does not guarantee capacity, however, and
since a major theme of the Obama presidency has been to
remedy America's strategic over-extension, it was important
that he could claim that other countries would do most of the
heavy lifting. France and Britain had pushed originally and
most enthusiastically for the air campaign, and if there was
a clear doctrine coming out of the Obama administration's
response, it had less to do with the conditions for humanitarian intervention than with a new style of American
leadership. 'American leadership is not simply a matter
of going it alone and bearing all of the burden ourselves',
Obama told the Nobel committee. 'Real leadership creates
the conditions and coalitions for others to step up as well; to
work with allies and partners so that they bear their share of
the burden and pay their share of the costs.' In an interview

with the *New Yorker's* Ryan Lizza, one administration official described this as a doctrine of 'leading from behind'.[46]
It was probably meant as a joke. Impolitic in any event, the
anonymous quote was a gift to the administration's critics
on the hawkish right. Yet, it was also reasonably accurate in
expressing administration hopes that US alliances and partnerships could be leveraged to promote peace and stability
without bankrupting the United States in the process. In the
specific case of Libya, however, the success of the doctrine
hinged on whether the French, British, other Europeans and
Arab partners were up to the challenge. It was a close call,
but the answer, in this case, turned out to be yes. Despite
Libyan rebels' evident disorganisation, NATO air power
was sufficient on its own to tip the balance against regime
forces. NATO suffered its own disunity, with German and
Polish abstentions, but workarounds for a coalition of the
willing led by Britain and France worked well enough.
British and French capability shortcomings were highlighted: although Europeans and Arabs conducted 75% of
combat sorties, they were utterly reliant on US refuelling,
intelligence, communications and, as the conflict dragged
on, munitions.[47] Yet, for assessing this Obama model of US
intervention, NATO's reliance on America's enabling infrastructure is not quite so damning an indictment as many
critics have alleged. The US infrastructure and resources
were, after all, available. For Washington, meanwhile, its
ownership stake and investment of diplomatic capital was
limited, while the actual marginal cost of US participation
has been estimated at around US$1bn – a rounding error in
the US defence budget.[48]

But did humanitarian intervention in Libya reinforce the far more expensive expectation that US military resources will be required for frequent, similar interventions elsewhere? The question rapidly became pertinent as Gadhafi's repression was replicated by the Assad regime in Syria. The problem was not, as often alleged, one of moral inconsistency: the accusation that intervening in Libya was somehow illegitimate because the US, France and Britain were not also intervening against repression in Syria, Bahrain, the Democratic Republic of the Congo (where there have in fact been EU-flagged troops), or even Saudi Arabia. The truth is that inconsistency is baked into the cake for as long as the American superpower lacks supernatural powers. Moreover, the set of problems amenable to outside military solutions is a small one. The urgent problem in Libya was not to create a democracy, which is not practical at gunpoint, but to prevent a massacre. That task was accomplished – no massacre took place after the intervention – and although it cannot be proven that, in the absence of intervention, a massacre would have taken place, the evidence, as suggested above, is strong. The NATO effort was helped, moreover, by geographic circumstance: Gadhafi's forces were battling the rebels along a narrow band of coastal communications north of the empty Sahara. Though it was so obvious at the time, this was a good place to apply air power. In Syria, by contrast, the social and physical landscape seems less amenable to effective intervention from the air.[49]

As this book went to press, Syria was continuing to use extreme violence against its people, pushing the country to the brink of civil war. Although Washington had little appetite for direct intervention, administration officials were aware that atrocities might become so overwhelming as to create extreme pressure for another humanitarian intervention. President Obama had already stated forcefully that solving the crisis would require the departure of Syrian President Bashar al-Assad from office. Although the president of the United States lacks the unlimited powers to make this happen, such statements tend to have consequences in terms of foreclosing diplomatic solutions that might over the long run leave the current regime in power. No certain outcome flows from such tendencies, and the long run could be very long indeed, but the underlying point is that there are plausible scenarios whereby an escalating US military engagement takes place. And if one considers the recent history of such engagements – Iraq, Bosnia, Kosovo, Afghanistan and most recently Libya – even tentative beginnings lead almost inexorably to regime change.

Counter-proliferation

We now know, of course, that while the Obama administration was debating whether to join a Libya intervention, it was also in the late stages of planning for a mission to kill Osama bin Laden. The concurrence of these operations serves to remind us that no single doctrine or tradition can really convey what America is up to or about. To borrow Walter Russell Mead's categories, a Wilsonian liberalism made it difficult for America to stand aloof from Libya's ordeal, while Jacksonian nationalism made it unlikely that Osama bin Laden, for all his success in evading capture, would end his days peacefully in bed.[50] The question that arises is whether the organised violence that is driven by either of these American traditions can fit comfortably into a template of strategic restraint.

In the matter of killing bin Laden, the answer is almost certainly yes. It is now an established historical fact that regimes, such as Afghanistan's pre-2001 Taliban, or individuals, such as Osama bin Laden, who are complicit in an attack on the United States, are very likely to be destroyed as a consequence. An offshore balancer with global reach can, if it applies its military power effectively and prudently, make it extremely costly for would-be foes to attack the direct interests or security of the United States. In the matter of Libya, the case was murkier. The ill-fated humanitarian intervention in Somalia of 1992–94 stood as a reminder of the risk that the US might be drawn into a stalemate, with Gadhafi's survival in power making America look, in Richard Nixon's immortal phrase, like a 'pitiful, helpless giant'. (Bin Laden often cited America's Somalia pullout as proof it was a paper tiger.[51]) It is not clear, however, that the immediate fall of Benghazi would have made America look much better than that. Some argued that NATO's support in toppling Gadhafi helped to insulate both Egypt and Tunisia from the consequences and contagion that would have resulted from Gadhafi's unchecked oppression. Military success in Libya hardly guarantees the success of democracy in the region – or, for that matter, in Libya – but it does buy more time for Egypt and Tunisia to consolidate their gains.

Were the US to be drawn into military support for the rebels in Syria, one matter for debate would be how the fall of Assad might feed into wider strategic calculations. Victory for the rebels would most likely mean the demise of Iran's only state ally in the region – a net plus for the United States. On the other hand, a protracted civil war could provide fields of mischief for Iran's Revolutionary Guard Corps and other promoters of terrorism, including Hizbullah and al-Qaeda affiliates. In any event, even Iran's greater isolation will not necessarily remove it as the major obstacle to the administration's stated ambition to 'return our posture in the region' to one 'far more in line with where we were before 1990'.[52] Simply put, it is hard to reconcile this desired retrenchment with the very real possibility that the United States will soon be drawn into another preventive war, perhaps sparked by Israeli air strikes against Iran's nuclear facilities.

Acts of preventive war do not always end in disaster. In 1981, Israeli planes destroyed the Iraqi reactor at Osirak – to loud international condemnation and quiet international relief. In 2007, the Israelis destroyed a nuclear facility in Syria; this time even the Syrians kept quiet. In 1967, for that matter, Israel launched what it had reason to consider a pre-emptive war against threatening Egyptian and Syrian forces, with what looked at the time to be salutary results (though the failure, after 43 years, to convert victory into a just peace with Palestinians has undermined if not squandered those results).

But Israel, in any event, is a special case. Born in trauma, besieged at birth and seeing itself as under attack ever since, it has rarely acted as though its highest priority was to preserve its stake in the stability or legitimacy of international order, because it never felt confident that it had been accepted into that order. Again, Israel itself shares some blame for this state of affairs. But the national psychology of forced isolation is not wholly detached from reality.

Here is one source of the gap between the Jerusalem way and the Washington way of imagining the consequences of military action against Iran's nuclear-enrichment capabilities. Israel's political leadership paints a picture of self-contained air strikes without a hugely damaging blowback. The picture is plausible. But one reason Washington doesn't believe it is that Washington has a much broader stake in the rules of international order. This statement may sound odd to those who look at America as the archetype of a superpower bull in the world's china shop. And it is true that the United States is generally inclined to a flexible reading of international law when it comes to judging its own use of force. Nonetheless, America sees itself – and has reason to see itself – as a main pillar of world order, with responsibilities that include, but certainly go far beyond, preventing Iran from developing a nuclear weapon. America's own excursion into preventive war is recent and regretted. The current administration can count many ways that US power was depleted through preventive action against an Iraqi threat that turned out to be more distant and hypothetical than was claimed at the time.

Both realists and pluralists will have the Iraq experience in mind as they warn against exaggerating the threat posed by Iran. Such warnings should be heeded. Today's strategists often aspire to have the paradigmatic influence of a George Kennan, but too rarely do they take on board the duality of Kennan's wisdom: his determination to avoid both wishful thinking about the nature of an adversary, and self-fulfilling panic about that adversary's intentions and capabilities. Kennan was accused of changing his mind about the severity of the Soviet threat, but in fact he was consistent. The challenge, as he saw it, was to face down and contain Soviet expansion without resorting to excessive militarisation or war – and without, moreover, trapping Stalin or his successors in a box such that *they* saw no alternative to war.

This raises comparisons to the Iranian problem worth thinking about. The argument that Iran cannot be contained without resorting to war is hard to fathom. The murderous, anti-Israel and anti-Semitic ranting of its regime cannot be ignored, but actual capabilities, disabilities and patterns of behaviour aimed at self-preservation also count. It is embarrassing even to address the Hitler analogy, but since Prime Minister Netanyahu and the American Right repeatedly raise it: Hitler presided over the strongest power in Europe; he conquered most of that continent with a military machine that threatened to subdue the Soviet Union and Britain, and might thereafter have been a match for the United States. Efforts to depict Iran as such a power collapse under any serious examination. Even the comparison to Cold War containment of the Soviets is misleading, largely because Iran is so much easier to contain. Iran is, in fact, weak and visibly weakening. The Arab Awakening might have given Tehran some initial hopes insofar as it threatened anti-Iranian Sunni regimes and toppled an American friend in Cairo. But the Gulf Arab regimes remain firmly in control, and Iran has proven irrelevant to the revolution in Egypt (even if that revolution may be moving in worrying directions from the Western perspective). Tehran's only ally in the Arab world is a besieged regime in Syria whose brutality is redounding to discredit the Iranians. When an Iranian commander threatened to close the Strait of Hormuz, the United States responded forcefully and Iran had to back down. Iran has terrorist proxies, but no serious military force in the region; against the US Fifth Fleet, it wields a collection of small boats. And with one possible exception, it does not have a message that resonates in the Arab world. That one exception is the plight of the Palestinians, but for now the Arabs are more concerned about their own conflicts and their own future. For the future, the plight of the Palestinians is something that the United States with Israel should be able to address.

Moreover, the Obama administration's success in international diplomacy to isolate Iran has been impressive. By mid-summer 2012, the European Union will not be consuming a drop of Iranian crude, having agreed to impose sanctions. For Iran's regime, the future looks grim: plummeting oil exports, a collapsing currency and banks that cannot operate abroad. The administration's working theory is that things will get so bad that the regime worries about its survival. Of course, it is only a theory that Tehran will respond to its predicament by seeking a negotiated settlement. The psychologically plausible alternative is that, seeing themselves practically at war, with regime survival at stake, Iran's leaders could resist showing any sign of weakness – and consider a willingness to negotiate as weakness. So, although crippling sanctions are what Israel wanted, and what the Obama administration succeeded in delivering, we cannot be sure that this will open an avenue to peace rather than bringing us closer to war. This is why the administration is taking every opportunity to remind the Iranians that it wants to avoid military conflict, is open to and desires a negotiated settlement. Whether this message is being received by a paranoid Iranian leadership is an open question. US politics does not help – during the Republican presidential nomination contest, all candidates except for Ron Paul were arguing that the United States should do everything Israel wants it to do, however belligerent, against Iran.

The capacity to undertake strategic reckonings of the costs as well as the benefits of resorting to force is a rock-bottom prerequisite for sustainable superpower. Yet America's ability to do so is complicated by its one truly 'special relationship'. It is a fact of political life and national affinities that America will pay extraordinary attention to Israel's definition of its own security predicament. (It is unfortunate that Israel, under its present government, seems less concerned about America's predicament.) The question is whether the United States can allow Israel's panic to override its own balance of risk and benefit from using military force against Iran.

As this book went to press, the Obama administration and the Netanyahu government were engaged in intense discussions about time lines and red lines. Regarding the former, Israel's political leadership (important Israeli intelligence and military figures dissent strongly) depicted a point of no return – presumably when sufficient enrichment centrifuges can be installed at an underground site near Qom. The US–Israeli gap here is possibly not so much one of threat perception per se, and more a difference in capabilities: American munitions might well be able to reach under that mountain, but the Israelis fear Iran's programme will soon reach the point where they cannot do anything about it themselves, and are entirely dependent on US action. Such dependence is hugely troubling for a country that has always insisted on maintaining autonomy over its own security. The Israelis are less concerned than Washington about the consequences of air attacks driving Iran to leave the Non-Proliferation Treaty and kick out International Atomic Energy Agency inspectors. For Israel, the NPT is simply the cover under which Iran continues towards a nuclear capability. Yet, from the US perspective, loss of the inspectors would indeed remove an important trip-wire between a latent nuclear capability and actual weaponisation.

This brings us to red lines. The Netanyahu government is not disposed to parse the distinction between actual nuclear weapons and latent capability based on enriched fissile material that has a theoretical – though in Iran's case, not much practical – justification in a civilian nuclear industry. The Obama administration, on the other hand, thinks the distinction is important. America's intelligence chiefs – CIA Director David Petraeus, and Director of National Intelligence James Clapper – both testified in February 2012 that they see no convincing evidence Tehran has made a definite decision to cross the threshold from a latent to an actual nuclear-weapons state.[53] The American case is that Iran can be prevented from crossing that threshold through continuing pressure, including the implicit threat of military action.

Israel might ask whether all the reasons for caution against a preventive attack now apply to attacking Iran at that weaponisation threshold as well? In some respects, the answer is yes. But deterrence often requires convincing an adversary that you are ready to throw caution to the wind. It would have made no rational sense to answer a movement of Soviet tanks into West Germany with nuclear weapons. But America was committed to doing so – a commitment that only made sense in the surreal realm of nuclear deterrence. Moreover, there is a powerful reason to believe that a military strike would make more sense at that point of weaponisation than it does now. As Mark Fitzpatrick, a non-proliferation expert at the IISS , puts it:

> A pre-emptive strike at a time when Iran is not on the verge of crossing the threshold and might still be dissuaded from doing so would surely create an Iranian determination to build nuclear weapons, and this time in secret. This problem of counter-productivity would no longer prevail if Iran had already decided to cross the line.[54]

So the red line argument is, on one level, about Israel's fear of being left alone and, on another level, about America, after wars in Iraq and Afghanistan, trying to find a more balanced and sustainable role for itself in the Middle East and beyond. This American rebalancing act is fraught with difficult questions about when it makes sense to use military force. Iran remains in brazen violation of multiple UN Security Council Resolutions regarding its enrichment programme;

the United States, as the 'pillar of international order', might be expected to do something about it. Such expectations are one reason that many American liberals, the present authors included, did not strongly oppose military action in the months leading up to the invasion of Iraq. But Iraq showed that, as much as letting rogues get away with systemic violations of UN demands, a superpower failing to respect its own limits can be corrosive to international stability as well as the domestic wellsprings of its own power. Can the United States can afford to engage in preventive war against every serious potential threat? By taking its role of 'world's policeman' too literally, the United States could easily get drawn into a succession of wars of counter-proliferation.

CHAPTER 3

Politics, polarisation and American exceptionalism

Understanding American power requires an exploration of two dynamics that currently drive the domestic politics of the United States: polarisation and exceptionalism. The story of polarisation deserves pride of place, because it defines in many ways how the United States now operates. It can be seen in the angry rhetoric of Fox News or MSNBC commentators and it explains why there is such ferocious conflict between the institutions of government. Any serious foreign-policy analysis must take account of these polemics. The debate about America's world role cannot be separated from its domestic debates about the proper nature and purpose of American society; responsibilities abroad cannot be separated from the question of income distribution at home. In a three-way trade-off between tax rates, social-welfare distribution (including health care) and national-security spending, none of the three can be treated as exogenous or taken for granted.

By contrast, the notion of exceptionalism lies deeper in the background and describes what the United States aspires to, more than how it functions. In theory, exceptionalism should be a point of consensus among Americans: the idea, borne partly of immigrant mythology, is that becoming American was and remains an active choice. Of course, the practice has been different, as 1960s black-power advocate Malcolm X and Obama's former pastor Jeremiah Wright implied. Americans argue fiercely over what it means to be exceptional, over which values should be celebrated, over how they have been honoured or shamed in the past, and over what should be done about it. Both of these dynamics are reflected in the remarkable socio-political phenomenon of the Tea Party.

Tea and liberty

One month into Obama's presidency, CNBC Business News Editor Rick Santelli became agitated while broadcasting from the floor of the Chicago Mercantile Exchange. He was indignant about the administration's emergency plans to help refinance millions of unpayable home mortgages that were a major cause of the financial crisis. 'The government is promoting bad behaviour', Santelli yelled. 'How about this, Mr President and new administration? Why don't you put up a website to have people vote … to see if we really want to subsidise the losers' mortgages?' The Chicago traders cheered, and after comparing Obama's 'collective' plans to what Castro had accomplished in Cuba, Santelli declared, 'We're thinking of having a Chicago Tea Party.'[1]

The 'Santelli rant' became a viral sensation on the Internet, and within weeks the 'Tea Party' movement had become a driving engine of right-wing reaction to the Obama presidency. The movement mainly overlapped with the conservative base of the Republican Party, but whereas that base previously was preoccupied with the cultural causes of the Christian Right – especially opposition to abortion and gay marriage – Tea Partiers agitated on a more secular and libertarian front against the 'socialist' threat that Obama posed to American liberties.[2] The Tea Partiers could appeal to a resonant historical fact: the United States had been founded, at least in part, as the consequence of a tax revolt (and the original Boston Tea Party was a rebellious cere-mony of throwing tea into Boston Harbor rather than paying newly imposed duties to drink it). But that was 235 years before Obama became president. The present-day Tea Party is driven by a visceral reaction against America as shaped by Franklin Roosevelt's New Deal. This reaction is not entirely new: the favoured Tea Party texts are the works of Ayn Rand, a screenwriter turned novelist who attracted a cult follow-ing after she published her major works, *The Fountainhead* (1943) and *Atlas Shrugged* (1957). Rand, an exile from revo-lutionary Russia, was in essence an inverted Marxist who argued that the true creators of value – capitalists, industri-alists, artists and scientists – needed to liberate themselves from exploitation by the masses of socio-economic inferi-ors, Santelli's 'losers'. Rand was also a radical atheist, a fact that might cause some dissonance in Republican ranks if it were widely known. But her central argument that any kind of redistribution was not just economically inefficient, but morally abhorrent, had become an animating idea of modern American conservatism.

In November 2010, just two years after Obama's elec-tion created such excitement, conservative Republicans rode back on a counter-wave. To hold onto majorities in Congress that his party had won in 2006 and improved in 2008, President Obama would have needed substantially improved economic conditions. This did not happen. Though most economists believed that the stimulus package of his first year had averted even greater disaster, it barely compensated for the spending cuts enacted by state and local governments that are legally obligated to try and balance their budgets even in a severe downturn. On 2 November 2010, election day, the US unemployment rate was a staggering 9.8%. The Republicans won 60 seats and took control of the House of Representatives. In the Senate, the Democrats lost six seats and narrowly held onto their majority. But the Senate was subject to a minority's blocking filibuster that required a super-majority of 60 votes to override. What had once been an occasionally invoked minority prerogative has evolved into a routine mechanism that has effectively ended majority rule and paralysed the Senate.[3]

The 2010 election constituted a stark repudiation of Obama's original promise that he could transcend the bitter polarisation of American politics.[4] The Tea Party triumph sharpened that polarisation – arguably the worst since the nineteenth century – in ways that could profoundly affect America's global projection of power and influence. Firstly, the Republican shift to the right – continuing a trend of some 20 years' standing – challenged the post-war consensus on what America was at home and should do abroad. It threatened to complicate or even repudiate the Obama experiment of rebranding America's offering in the global marketplace of ideas about politics and strategy. In other words, the

Republicans' continued drift rightward presents a version of American Exceptionalism considerably more strident than that put forward by the George W. Bush administration, a version that would be very difficult for the rest of the world to swallow.[5] Secondly, and more concretely, political paralysis in the midst of the worst economic crisis since the Great Depression has cast some doubt on the American capacity to either fully revive its domestic political economy or finance its global commitments.[6]

Contested exceptionalism

The overriding critique from his Republican opponents consisted of the claim that Obama did not believe in an innate American exceptionalism. In domestic policy, he was trying to turn America against its nature into a version of 'socialist' Europe.[7] Leaving aside whether wealthy European democracies should be considered socialist dystopias, there was a real problem in claiming that the huge market failures that the president tried to fix – financial meltdown after a housing bubble, and a health-insurance market that excluded tens of millions – should really be considered the sources of American greatness. Still, the Republican arguments resonated, insofar as American exceptionalism probably did have to be defined as a contrast to those societies America most resembled. And maybe the rough-and-tumble excitement of American society would be flattened if made to conform to more staid European traditions.[8] It is just difficult to imagine the circumstances under which that would happen.

In foreign policy, the charge relied mainly on taking egregiously out of context something Obama had said at a press conference in Strasbourg early in his administration, in response to a question about whether he believed in the concept of American exceptionalism. 'I believe in American exceptionalism, just as I suspect that the Brits believe in British exceptionalism and the Greeks believe in Greek exceptionalism.'[9] The critics pounced with the rejoinder – logical enough in itself – that an exceptionalism that other countries could claim as well was hardly very exceptional. They invariably failed to acknowledge the rest of Obama's reply, which started with 'I'm enormously proud of my country and its role and history in the world' and ended with a lengthy discourse on ways in which the United States has been a unique force for progress and decency. Obama's answer partook of the secular case that historical circumstance, political genius and moral tradition have endowed the United States with a special and, on balance, benign role, most evident in the twentieth century. He did not make the case that the United States is exceptional by dint of divine ordination, as implied by many of his Republican critics, but he does not sound very different from writers like Robert Kagan (as discussed elsewhere in this volume).

The Obama–Kagan secular argument is debatable, while the Republicans' case is a theological proposition beyond the expertise of the present authors. There is, however, one very compelling aspect of American exceptionalism that is embodied in Obama's presidency. There are few countries in the world that would be likely to elevate a member of a recently oppressed minority to be head of state or government. (Though important exceptions should be acknowledged: both Austria and France had post-war prime ministers who were Jewish and, in the Austrian case, at least, Bruno Kreisky was popular and remains deeply respected.) If the cathartic effects of Obama's 2008 election victory had faded by 2012, the fact of his presidency nonetheless continued to demonstrate America's progress in the 50 years since Obama was born. Not only did it say something immensely attractive about the American electorate, it could also serve as a powerful emblem of the American democratic pluralism that is worthy of global emulation.

Beyond the uniquely important – and difficult – experience of African-Americans, America could claim a broader tradition of immigrant assimilation that not only constituted an enduring element of the American creed, but also had continuing positive consequences in terms of American demographic and economic dynamism. And American inclusiveness extended to the religious diversity that President George W. Bush recognised as a valuable American asset immediately after 11 September, when he made notable gestures to persuade American Muslims that they were valued citizens and not under suspicion as fifth columnists for jihadist terror. Unfortunately, these gestures were undermined by the perhaps inevitable mobilisation of US immigration services in sweeping up Muslims for minor visa violations in the fearful aftermath of the terrorist catastrophe, by the Manichean terms of a declared war on terrorism and, most corrosively, by the decision to use coercive methods including torture – in both legal and common-sense definitions – against terrorist suspects.

The Tea Party movement also included an uglier turn against the more darkly complexioned and more culturally and religiously complicated America that this dynamism was producing and that Obama himself reflected. A panic about illegal immigration, mainly from Mexico and other parts of Latin America, had already manifested during the 2008 Republican primaries, forcing John McCain to abandon his traditional support for generous treatment of undocumented immigrants, and severely threatening the project of President Bush's political architect, Karl Rove, for turning a significant portion of the Hispanic electorate Republican. By 2010 this reaction was reflected in both Republican political rhetoric and draconian laws in states such as Arizona intended to make life miserable for illegal immigrants and, it was hoped, encourage their 'self-deportation'.

In the summer of 2010, meanwhile, there emerged a significant current of anti-Muslim hysteria that was both new and manifestly at odds with President George W. Bush's efforts, nine years earlier, to discourage such a backlash. An especially hysterical argument was set off by the proposal of a leading Muslim proponent of moderate dialogue, Faisal Abdul Rauf, to build the Cordoba Center, a mosque and cultural centre at 45–51 Park Place, just two blocks from the site of the destroyed World Trade Center. The media storm over the 'Ground Zero Mosque' – which was more than a mosque and not really at Ground Zero – had been set off by a series of 'tweets' (messages sent via the social networking site Twitter) from Sarah Palin, the 2008 Republican candidate for vice president, to her followers. These included a call that 'Peaceful New Yorkers, pls refute the Ground Zero Mosque plan if you believe catastrophic pain caused @ Twin Towers site is too raw, too real'. Former House Speaker Newt

Gingrich joined in by comparing the idea of a mosque near Ground Zero to Nazi signs at Washington DC's Holocaust Museum.

In March 2011, two months after launching a bid for the Republican presidential nomination, Gingrich also joined the battle against imposition of sharia law in the United States. Though one might imagine that this spectre would rank fairly low on the list of clear and present dangers to the American republic, at least 18 states considered legislation in 2010 and 2011 to prevent judges from exercising their – so far, well concealed – plans to replace Anglo-Saxon jurisprudence with an Islamic substitute. Gingrich portrayed a titanic conflict: 'I am convinced that if we do not decisively win the struggle over the nature of America, by the time [my grandchildren are] my age they will be in a secular atheist country, potentially one dominated by radical Islamists and with no understanding of what it once meant to be an American.'[10] Though the juxtaposition – atheist and Islamist – might seem puzzling, liberal blogger Matthew Yglesias observed that it made sense if one appreciated that the essential anxiety into which Gingrich was tapping consisted of white conservatives' fears about their fading ethno-cultural landscape.[11] The 'birther' obsessions of numerous conservatives, which inferred that Obama had lied about his birthplace and thereby his citizenship, was also more explainable in the context of this anxiety.

All of which raises the question of lingering racism in the right-wing reaction to Obama and Obama's America. Certainly a candidate like Gingrich showed that he was happy to resort to racist code-words when it suited his purposes: a favourite, during his presidential campaign, was to repeatedly call Obama 'the food-stamp president'. Before announcing his candidacy, the former House Speaker embraced the barely coded thesis of conservative writer Dinesh D'Souza, published by *Forbes Magazine*, and turned into a book titled *The Roots of Obama's Rage*.[12] The essential argument was that the American president was endowed with radical, anti-American socialism by the anti-colonial rage of his Kenyan father. In truth, Obama met his father only once after Obama Snr left the family when his son was a toddler: the president was raised by Kansans, not Kenyans. Yet, for Gingrich, the D'Souza thesis embodied a 'stunning' and 'profound' insight. 'What if [Obama] is so outside our comprehension, that only if you understand Kenyan, anti-colonial behavior, can you begin to piece together [his actions]?' Gingrich asked. 'That is the most accurate, predictive model for his behavior.'[13] It took a former George W. Bush speechwriter, David Frum, to state the obvious about Gingrich's rhetoric: 'When last was there such a brazen outburst of race-baiting in the service of partisan politics at the national level? George Wallace took more care to sound race-neutral.'[14]

Gingrich was hardly alone in making such arguments among prominent Republicans. For several years, starting well before Obama's election as president, Rush Limbaugh warned his listeners incessantly that Obama's primary purpose in life and politics was to punish American whites for the racial sins of their forefathers. Mike Huckabee, the former Arkansas governor who ran for president in 2008 and was leading in the Republican polls for 2012 until he decided not to run, speculated in a radio interview that Obama must have internalised a 'Mau Mau' worldview while growing up in Kenya. (Huckabee later said he 'misspoke' and meant to say Indonesia, where Obama had indeed spent some years as a child, though how he was supposed to have adhered in Indonesia to the Mau Mau revolt in Kenya was left unexplained.)[15]

The argument here is not that the angry reaction to Obama is driven primarily by racism. In terms of Republican and Tea Party politics, such an argument would be undermined if not refuted by the fact that Herman Cain, a conservative black businessman, was also for a brief period in 2011 leading polls for the Republican nomination. Likewise, Mike Huckabee's unfortunate pandering to prejudices over Obama's Kenyan roots should be balanced against his moving defence of Jeremiah Wright – the minister of Obama's Chicago church who got candidate Obama into some trouble during the 2008 presidential campaign when videos of incendiary sermons circulated. ('I grew up in a very segregated South,' said Huckabee about Wright's anger. 'And I think that you have to cut some slack'.[16]) There is, moreover, no reason to suspect Newt Gingrich of personal racism. That said, it is impossible to ignore the repeated use of racialist dog-whistle tactics by prominent Republicans, whatever their personal convictions. Ultimately, the evidence indicates that important conservative political leaders believe that stigmatising the president for his black otherness can pay dividends at the polls. They are not likely to be completely misinformed about this: certainly a significant white minority harbours real racial resentment. And yet, for a president whose tenure coincided with dire economic conditions, Obama remained remarkably popular.

The racial dimension to America's political polarisation is, in other words, complicated.[17] Without doubt, both the twentieth-century struggle over racial segregation and the nineteenth-century civil war over slavery hardened sectional dividing lines that remain important in contemporary American politics. Paradoxically, however, America's acute problem of political polarisation also stems systemically from its immense progress towards racial enlightenment – and not merely, or even primarily, due to the Limbaugh brand of white backlash. To understand the current systemic problem, it is instructive to compare the American antagonisms of 2012 to the political and social turmoil of the 1960s.

On one level, the 1960s tumult was far more dramatic. It was the decade of assassinations, lynchings and race riots, Vietnam protests and campus unrest, and a Maoist-tinged domestic terrorism on the fringes of the American version of 1968 protests. This decade was followed by the constitutional crisis of Watergate, into which all sorts of personal and political enmities between Richard Nixon and his enemies were poured. And yet, throughout these years it was still possible, at the level of politics, to maintain a working consensus on the purposes and operations of government. Part of the paradox is that even as the civil-rights movement advanced, the remaining structures of segregation helped that consensus function.

The Democratic Party at the time was a ramshackle coalition that included Southern segregationists and Northern and Midwestern liberals. The Republican Party included a substantial share of pro-civil rights moderates and liberals, as well as the New Right conservatives such as Barry Goldwater. These were the variegated ideological conditions that allowed President Lyndon B. Johnson to fashion bipartisan majorities for such landmark legislation as the 1964 Civil Rights Act. But the majorities themselves were a victim of his success. Over the ensuing generation, Southern conservative Democrats moved steadily from the Democratic Party to the Republican Party. As the latter became more and more conservative, liberals and moderates found it less and less congenial. As a consequence, the racial divisions in American politics aligned themselves with the major economic and social divisions as well – with a 'colour blind' coalition of conservatives on the right and a 'race conscious' coalition of progressives on the left.[18]

Fiscal paralysis

The most immediate and direct consequence of this polarisation was to frustrate the dual project of both reflating a depressed economy and charting a plausible course of restored fiscal balance. The problem of overspending equally can be seen as a problem of under-taxing. 'Tax revolts' of the 1970s – notably a California ballot initiative requiring legislative supermajorities to raise property taxes – came together with ideological and economic arguments that high marginal income-tax rates were disincentives to economic activity. This made sense in regard to the very high marginal rates – over 90% – that prevailed during the immediate post-war period and through the Kennedy administration. It may also have applied to the 70% top rate that prevailed until

Ronald Reagan's 1981 tax reform.[19] But there is a point below which the a reduction in the top marginal tax rate will no longer add either to revenues or to market incentives. The famous 'Laffer curve' popularised by conservative economist Arthur Laffer claims to plot the relationship between tax rates and revenues gathered. It is shaped like an upside-down bowl with the highest point in the middle, where the top marginal tax rate is set to maximise both revenue and growth.

The problem is to find that sweet spot in the relationship between taxes and economic performance; there is much disagreement about the precise rate of tax that provides maximal revenue and growth. The first Reagan tax reform is widely touted by Republicans as a big step in the right direction. In fact, however, Reagan's tax policy turned out to be a perfect recipe for the US federal government to run large fiscal deficits on the back of huge increases in defence spending.[20] The deficit did, to be sure, help get the country out of recession for simple Keynesian reasons: increased government spending, notably defence spending, and lower taxes. Reagan himself, although he was to become an icon of the anti-tax movement, followed his initial package of 'supply-side' tax cuts with some major tax *increases* in the 1986 tax reform to repair the fiscal damage. He also appointed a commission to propose reforms that would shore up the solvency of Social Security, the American state pensions system, and was able to work with the Democratic House Speaker, Thomas 'Tip' O'Neill, to get the reforms implemented. Ideological currents in both parties remained fluid enough for such cooperation to work.

It was in the 1990s, under the leadership of Newt Gingrich, that the modern Republican Party took shape as a more conservative movement dedicated to progressively lower marginal tax rates. Reagan's successor, George H.W. Bush, was vilified as an apostate for violating his 'read my lips' pledge in the 1988 campaign against any new taxes. Right-wing anger at this broken promise contributed to his 1992 defeat by Bill Clinton, who returned the federal government to solvency with a combination of tax rises, budget cuts and healthy growth. The George W. Bush administration, moderate by the standards of today's Republicans, nonetheless reduced marginal tax rates again, ostensibly to deal with the problem of a government budget surplus. The legislation included a ten-year expiry date, at which point taxes were to revert back to Clinton-era levels, so the cuts could be scored as more affordable. But the administration had always assumed and planned for their extension. The anti-tax position was locked in by the authority of conservative political entrepreneur Grover Norquist, who has long campaigned for a smaller federal government.[21] Since 1986, Norquist had demanded a written pledge from every Republican candidate never to vote for a tax increase, or even a tax reform that increased net revenues.[22] By 2010, all but a handful of House and Senate Republicans had signed it.

The Bush tax cuts, together with increased defence spending and wars in Afghanistan and Iraq, once again locked large structural deficits into the federal budget. Economic collapse in 2008–09 meant plummeting revenues that hugely worsened the imbalance, as did the stimulus spending that was required to avert a catastrophic depression. With

Republicans' victory in the 2010 elections, further counter-cyclical spending, though urgently needed, became almost impossible. Obama was able to trade a two-year extension of upper-income tax cuts for a $238 billion 'mini-stimulus' of extended unemployment benefits and a payroll-tax holiday. (The upper-income tax-cut extension had some stimulus benefit as well.) But the new power balance in Washington helped shift the debate from the current economic emergency to a potential future one. Washington was seized by the notion that the federal government's debt and deficit constituted the most urgent crisis facing the United States. The perverse policy implication was that the United States faced a fiscal emergency of such proportions that it should respond to a collapse of economic demand by cutting demand further.

Yet the United States was not insolvent in any common-sense meaning of the term. Though there were repeated warnings that bond markets might lose confidence in US Treasuries, the federal government's actual borrowing costs remained very low. Moreover, its medium-term budget deficit would be mostly erased if Washington returned to Clinton-era tax rates – as current law in fact mandates to happen at the end of Obama's first term. Letting all Bush tax cuts expire at the end of 2012 would cut $3.9 trillion off the national debt by 2020, reducing the deficit to about 2.5% of GDP, meaning, under reasonable economic conditions, the debt would no longer be growing faster than the economy. Thus, the fundamental problem was political and ideological: the fact that one of the two major political parties in the United States has adopted the position that in an already historically low-taxed country, it was nonetheless a matter of unyielding dogma that taxes must always go down and never up. Operating according to such dogma could indeed bankrupt the country. But such a disaster would be caused by a somewhat surreal political refusal to pay for the basic needs of an advanced democratic welfare state, rather than by America living beyond its means.[23]

The United States also faces a significant long-term budget and debt problem beyond 2020. If one could erase the effects of the tax cuts, and discount the costs of two wars, there would remain the genuinely difficult problem of health-care costs for the elderly, which drives most of the long-term deficit. In theory, these costs should be containable – after all, Canada and most rich European countries spend considerably less on health care with better results. In practice, given the hybrid nature of an American system that combines private insurance with a huge socialised protection for the elderly, there was strong resistance to imposing the kind of centralised cost controls that have succeeded, at least in relative terms, in Europe and Canada. Enactment of the Obama health-care reform did in fact offer some help in controlling these costs. The institution of near universal coverage – a liberal goal starting with President Harry Truman – was paid for through imposing an 'individual mandate' requiring all citizens to purchase health insurance (with subsidies to help those who otherwise could not afford to do so). This should make the overall system sounder by bringing in premiums from millions of relatively healthy adults who had heretofore been 'free-riders' on a system under which hospital emergency rooms were required by law to treat them (though only for emergencies – this requirement is in no way a substitute for universal health care).

The new health-care law also turned private medical insurance companies into public utilities insofar as they would now be required to insure everyone at comparable rates, regardless of pre-existing conditions or demographic risk factors. And the law contained a large number of measures designed to 'bend the curve' of rising medical costs, especially in Medicare-covered treatment for the elderly. By themselves, however, the reforms did not solve the cost problem. In any event, Republican presidential candidates have promised to repeal the reforms if elected,[24] even though the Obama health-care reforms that Tea Party critics excoriated as a dangerous encroachment on freedom were very similar to – indeed, partly modelled on – the plan that Republican presidential front-runner Mitt Romney had proudly implemented in Massachusetts when he was governor there.

By summer 2011, America's political polarisation raised the spectre of a new financial crisis. The proximate cause was an arcane feature of federal budgeting, whereby the Congress that appropriates spending has to hold a separate vote to authorise the debt to cover it. In the past that second vote was routine – since the debt is obviously created by the spending in excess of revenue, not the debt 'authority' – even if some legislators used it to grandstand against the causes of the debt, as indeed Obama himself had done when voting as a senator against raising the debt ceiling. But it was innovative for a newly elected House majority to attempt to use the debt-ceiling authority as pressure to impose its policy choices. Controlling just one house of Congress, with Democrats in charge of the Senate and the White House, conservatives nevertheless claimed a mandate to impose their vision of how to close the budget gap. Their vision was in fact not all that specific, except in one respect: it had to include zero new revenues.[25]

The predicted consequences of the US government defaulting on its debt, for even a day, ranged from dire to catastrophic. That debt would almost certainly be down-graded by credit-rating agencies, resulting in increased borrowing costs – already a massive share of the budget – and a return to technical recession was very possible if not extremely likely. There were fears that the global financial system would seize up as it had in 2008, and this new finan-cial crisis was threatened at a time when several European countries were teetering on the brink of their own sovereign debt debacles. Another systemic crisis was possible.

Under these circumstances of high-stakes blackmail, Obama's increasingly numerous liberal critics were aston-ished that he would enter into policy negotiations at all. It seemed to them a wiser course for the president to insist that the debt ceiling was a purely technical issue, albeit an immensely grave one, which he refused to link to policy ques-tions at all. This was the practice of the past, and it would, they argued, put the entire onus of risking US government creditworthiness on the Republicans, who would presum-ably want to avoid responsibility for the consequences. But it eventually became clear that Obama saw this as an opportu-nity to strike a 'grand bargain' to remove the long-term debt overhang. He was willing to concede a great deal of liberal spending for a pact that would make liberal governance more practical in the future. To this end, he held private talks with the Republican House Speaker, John Boehner, who was also attracted to the idea, and they discussed the rough outlines of an ambitious debt reduction: roughly $4tr over ten years. The package was heavily skewed towards Republican preferences, about $4 in spending cuts for every $1 in increased revenue.

The negotiations collapsed after it was clear that Boehner would not be able to bring his Tea Party class of conservatives to vote for the deal. When it came to revenue increases, they told him, zero meant zero. Some conservatives also expressed doubt about predictions of default and financial crisis. By the middle of July, Boehner and his Senate counterpart, Minority Leader Mitch McConnell, were showing signs of panic: it did not appear that they could control their members.

The crisis was partly averted, but not solved. Adamant that a deficit-reduction package could include no tax increases, the Republican-controlled House agreed at the 11th hour to raise the debt ceiling on the basis of setting up a bipartisan 'super committee' that would be tasked to reach a long-term budget agreement. If it failed, large automatic spending reductions would, under the agreement, be brought to bear equally upon domestic and defence spending – the idea being that this would give left and right equal incentive to bargain seriously.

With failure to reach a long-term agreement, Standard & Poor's (S&P) downgraded the US government's credit rating to from AAA to AA+, specifically blaming 'the gulf between the political parties' for reducing confidence that Washington would be able to get its finances in order. In fact, as Binyamin Appelbaum and Eric Dash of the *New York Times* wrote at the time, S&P was 'acting in the face of evidence that investors consider[ed] Treasuries among the safest investments in the world'.[26] The disaster did not come to pass. Yields on US Treasuries remained low following the S&P downgrade (which was not followed by Moody's and Fitch, the other major ratings agencies). On the other hand, US economic growth, which had been recovering slowly, stalled again – and many economic analysts blamed the debt-ceiling debacle in Washington for at least part of this slowdown. The super committee, meanwhile, went on to hit the same conservative wall – no tax increases whatsoever – and duly failed. The automatic budget cuts were scheduled to take effect in early 2013.

Money and morals

This prospect was interesting, because it might have forced the American conservatives to confront some basic arithmetic: a large military establishment, and the world role it enables, must be paid for through either taxes or borrowing (which generally requires future taxes). The theoretical alternative, gutting the welfare state, would run into both practical and moral difficulties. In practical terms, the largest share of federal spending goes to health care for the elderly, a key constituency for Republicans who have promised to preserve Medicare spending without cuts. They might be tempted to imagine that Medicaid, the health programme covering the poor which also makes up a large share of federal spending, would offer an easier target. In fact, more than two-thirds of Medicaid spending goes for the elderly and long-term disabled.[27] After excluding Medicare, Medicaid, interest payments on the federal debt, and defence spending, what is left is simply too small to cover existing deficits.

In any event, the modern welfare state is one of the great accomplishments of post-War capitalist democracies. This is a moral judgement, but in truth any system for financing a global strategic role implies fundamental moral and political choices. In theory, one might imagine the United States as a kind of Spartan superpower, exerting power abroad while accepting degradation and decay as part of the human condition at home. In practice, however, a divided, stagnant political economy will not provide the material basis for sustainable global power. This is a theme we will return to later in this volume.

Exceptionalism is the narrative through which Americans explain to themselves why it is their obligation and privilege to act as the world's policeman. If the idea of exceptionalism is turned into a source of ridicule rather than strength, the rest of the world – much of which has welcomed, accepted, or at least acquiesced in the special American role – will do so no longer. Extreme solipsism on the part of US elites – a discourse that is increasingly divorced from the world's real problems – would seem likely to hasten that rejection.

If, for example, serious concerted action by a global community to curb CO_2 emissions does not begin within the next 20 years, the world could face global temperature rises and climate changes that would be potentially catastrophic and almost certainly irreversible for a span of centuries. This, arguably, makes climate change one of the few overriding moral and strategic problems of our time. As recently as 2008, Republican Senator John McCain ran for president touting a market-based 'cap and trade' scheme to curtail carbon emissions, as did his chief competitor for the Republican nomination, Mitt Romney. Two years later, it was obligatory dogma for all Republican presidential candidates to deny that global warming was taking place, or that humankind had anything to do with it, or – in the most moderate version – that it could be remotely worth the cost in economic liberty to do anything about it. There is no mainstream conservative party in any other major democracy that propounds remotely similar views. Even if President Obama is re-elected in 2012, he will face Congressional terrain that could make it impossible to return in a serious way to this issue, which had been one of his legislative priorities at inauguration. And if the United States – the world's largest economy and the second-largest per capita producer of greenhouse gases among the major economies – does not help lead a global community towards a solution, then a solution would appear to be highly unlikely.

If, to take another example, the US government continues to promote an agreement that ends Israel's occupation regime over Palestinians, it may fail. The United States and its Israeli ally face genuinely difficult dilemmas in this regard. But some 20 years ago a Republican president, George H.W. Bush, exerted serious pressure on the Israeli government to curtail Jewish settlements in occupied territory. Twenty years later, Bush's political heirs label as 'appeasement' any effort to nudge Israel in the direction of peace. Gingrich during the campaign called the Palestinians an 'invented people'. (This statement had some historical validity in the same sense that Americans obviously constitute a self-invented nation – and a relatively young one at that – but Gingrich's clear purpose was to dismiss Palestinian aspirations for political power over their own lives on the territories that they call home.) Mitt Romney says it is 'throwing Israel under a bus' for the US president to repeat the position of every US administration since Lyndon B. Johnson's: an end to colonising settlements and a peace agreement based on 1967 borders, with mutually agreed adjustments.

Meanwhile, Washington works hard with both Israel and Arab states to contain Iranian power, Tehran's support for terrorism, and its implied nuclear threat. It may remain true that Arab regimes, mostly fearful of Iran, will support this effort, regardless of what happens to Palestinians. It should be noted, however, that this is a status quo arrangement dependent upon the continued stifling of Arab democracy, as well as a lack of political power among Palestinians in Israel-controlled territory. If a Republican president pursues policies towards Israel that Republican candidates say they will pursue, the gap between American behaviour and American ideals will become wider.

These examples – a just and lasting Israel–Palestine peace, and action against global warming – may be seen as 'liberal' priorities today, but the point is that until very recently they were considered bipartisan and mainstream priorities. Perhaps they will be so again. Reconstituting a 'vital centre' is necessary for restoring balance to foreign policy as well as domestic affairs. The Republican leadership has moved to the hard right in response to a constituency that appears agitated by both economic difficulty and demographic change: the America that these constituents felt part of is rapidly fading, and their economic future looks unpromising. But economic conditions can improve, while the Republican Party will need to broaden its appeal in order to avoid demographic marginalisation. This might happen quickly: the Mitt Romney who styled himself a 'progressive' Republican governor of Massachusetts might conceivably revert to this recent form if he wins the presidential election. His strident (and utterly false) refrain accusing Obama of constantly 'apologising' for America might be forgotten if he were to defeat Obama and then take on the responsibility for presenting US power, with all of its unavoidably rough edges, to the rest of the world.

A kinder, gentler American exceptionalism is in the logic that best fits the American national interest. It could reasonably be argued that Obama was naturally more cautious about asserting American superiority to foreign audiences. George W. Bush had run for president promising to present a more humble face to the world, and no one thought to accuse him of being ashamed of his country.

Then again, the foreign policy of Bush turned out to be altogether different from what he promised in the 2000 presidential campaign. Part of this difference was due to the tragic events of 9/11. It was clear even before that terrible day, however, that Bush was going to be more partisan and more assertive than either his campaign rhetoric or his predecessors such is the effect of polarisation in American politics. Some 12 years later and under the pressure of the global economic and financial crisis, that influence has waxed and not waned.

CHAPTER FOUR

The causes and consequences of austerity

Perceptions can be distorted in a crisis. Historical perspective suffers the most. In this, Robert Kagan may be right to argue that:

> one recession, or even a severe economic crisis, need not mean the beginning of the end of a great power. The United States suffered deep and prolonged economic crises in the 1890s, the 1930s, and the 1970s. In each case, it rebounded in the following decade and actually ended up in a stronger position relative to other powers than before the crisis. The 1910s, the 1940s, and the 1980s were all high points of American global power and influence.[1]

It is certainly possible that the United States will rise from this current slump to another apogee of power and influence. Given the political dysfunction described in the last chapter, however, it is difficult now to see that path to renewed confidence. Prerequisite would be to understand the nature of the economic and financial crisis well enough to engineer an appropriate remedy both for the effects it has in the present and for the risk that it may recur. Here, however, there is an unnerving absence of a basic consensus about how the economy works and how it can be repaired. The traditional Keynesian models endorsed by mainstream economists are correct in general and indispensable in particular for understanding and counteracting the kinds of catastrophic slumps that major economies suffered in the 1930s and are suffering today. These models require counter-cyclical demand management through both central-bank monetary policy and government spending. On the fiscal side, this means accumulating budget surpluses in times of strong economic growth and accepting – in fact welcoming – deficits at times of economic contraction. Unfortunately, counter-cyclical is also counter-intuitive: most voters, and many politicians, follow the gut-level wisdom that governments are like households, and should tighten their belts when times are tough. Against such apparent common sense, the Keynesian narrative of economic history – a narrative shared by President Obama and his advisers – has struggled with only limited success. In much of Europe, the anti-Keynesian narrative has proven even stronger. If, as we believe, the contending prescription of austerity to fight recession-bloated deficits and government debt is not only ineffective but makes the problem worse, then a dark shadow blots the prospects of the United States and its major European partners to recover economic confidence and international influence.[2]

For the long run, of course, Kagan may be right about American potential for regeneration, but the long run, as John Maynard Keynes famously observed, 'is a misleading guide'.[3] Moreover, longer-term considerations also bring us to the other side of the ledger: the need to accumulate fiscal surpluses in times of growth, and to achieve sustainable balance among global economies. The imbalances that prevailed – most notably between China and the US – prior to the crisis are complex in their causes, but it is reasonable to worry, or at least to inquire, about their relation to chronic fiscal deficits and overspending. This inquiry raises, in turn, the question of how the United States has financed, and will continue to finance, its world role. In any event, these daunting problems – recovery for the present, balance for the future – require a basic understanding of how we fell into the ongoing crisis.

The road to ruin

There are, roughly speaking, two kinds of recessions. The first is tied to the business cycle and consists of a period of fast growth and accelerating inflation followed by a period of slower growth and rising unemployment. The United States has suffered through ten such recessions since the Second World War, sometimes in unfortunate synchronicity with its major European and Japanese trading partners.[4]

The second kind of recession is worse. The basic pattern is the same as found in a cyclical recession, but it includes an important difference related to the excessive movement of asset prices. Asset prices expand during the boom period into speculative bubbles on the basis of a pervasive belief that the prices will continue rising. When these bubbles burst during the subsequent downturn, they reveal an economy that was dangerously over-indebted on the basis of imagined wealth. The wealth suddenly vanishes; the debts remain. Hence, what follows is a sharp reversal of fortunes as self-fulfilling pessimism replaces irrational exuberance because households and businesses shift from borrowing to saving. The cumulative effect of these decisions is to make everyone worse off. The 'paradox of thrift', identified by Keynes, is that this new-found propensity to save, rational and even virtuous though it may be for individuals, is disastrous for the economy as a whole. The attendant bank failures and balance-sheet impairment take a long time to fix.

The distortions are not exactly symmetrical, but they are closely correlated, up and down. Generally speaking, the more irrational and exaggerated the bubble, the more savage and panic-stricken the reversal. Such was the dynamic of the Great Depression of the 1930s, and it returned with a vengeance in the final years of the last decade.[5]

In 2007, the asset was real estate and the housing-market bubble was inflated by capital inflows from China, easy mortgage credit in the United States, and practically unregulated financial markets that devised ever more complex instruments to bundle and 'securitise' mortgage assets.[6] Risk assessments for these securities were based on mathematical models that factored in just about every conceivable data point and price relationship except one: the possibility of a general and sustained fall in house prices.[7] No one seemed to worry how mortgage borrowers could pay off their loans, because no one seemed able to imagine that house prices would stop rising.

This failure of imagination arguably was compounded by the way that home-ownership has developed in the United States in response to the closing off of other opportunities for personal economic success. Put another way, and somewhat ironically, the housing bubble was resilient because the underlying US economic performance was so weak and the distribution of gains across winners and losers was so inequitable. Job growth had been slower than population growth throughout the George W. Bush administration; the civilian labour force grew by 8% from 2000 to 2008 while civilian employment grew by just 6% over the same period.[8] Meanwhile, income inequality continued to widen, casting dark shadows across the American dream of upward mobility.[9]

Bricks and mortar offered a way out. Ubiquitous wealth appeared to be available in real estate. Following the contraction of the information-technology bubble of the 1990s, the US economy was revived and expanded by a second speculative bubble in housing prices. Low interest rates, a conscious policy response to the risk that panic after 11 September would throttle the economy, helped feed the frenzy. In *The Big Short*, Michael Lewis gives a compelling account of the near-manic psychology of borrowers, lenders and even credit-rating agencies in this period. Lewis makes it clear that various degrees of abusive lending and fraud also played a role in the sale of mortgages to so-called sub-prime borrowers (a reference to the borrower's low credit-worthiness).[10]

Lenders were complacent, even reckless, because in their imagined worst case they were happy to lay claim to the assets (houses) backing the loans. The complacency extended to financial markets that were busy constructing a great pyramid of leverage through the creation of the complex securities. These Collateralised Debt Obligations (CDOs) packaged together mortgages of different types and qualities to provide investors with a variety of different risk-related rates of return. The credit-rating agencies routinely awarded these securities high marks without adequate concern for or attention to what the securities contained and how they would be regarded by investors. Worse, as more and more of these securities flowed across financial markets, the unknowns they carried with them metastasised. No one could quite figure out what share of financial institutions' balance sheets was subprime and few bothered to make the effort. The answer mattered little so long as house prices continued rising rather than falling.[11]

But in 2006 and 2007, as mortgage defaults increased and the prices for mortgage-backed securities declined, financial institutions looked at one another warily. Since the extent of the risk was unknowable, interbank lending – an indispensable lubricant of international finance – started to freeze up. Among the first casualties in summer 2007 were German regional banks, IKB and Sachsen LB, and French banking giant BNP Paribas, which froze redemptions on some of its large investment funds. Weeks later, British mortgage lender Northern Rock called for special liquidity from the Bank of England (BoE). Once the BoE announced that fact to the markets, Northern Rock experienced a bank run and the British government had to step to nationalise the bank.

The crisis quickly spread beyond the housing finance sector. As mortgage-backed securities suffered increasing losses in the second half of 2007, banks stopped lending to each other and economic growth slowed sharply. On 22 January 2008 the Federal Reserve announced a 75 basis point (0.75 percentage point) cut in its base rate of interest in response to a massive sell-off on Wall Street. This was the largest single cut in more than 20 years. Major American and foreign banks were forced into large write-downs of the value of their assets, and had to turn to the markets for new funding to bolster their capital buffers and avoid bankruptcy. In March 2008 it emerged that the crisis was also affecting US investment bank Bear Stearns. To avert a panic and ensure liquidity, the Federal Reserve made another 75 basis point reduction in its policy rates while organising a JPMorgan Chase buyout of Bear Stearns for much less than the $170 price at which the shares had been trading the previous year. But interbank lending remained tight. Other institutions showed the strains, and in the first week of September, 'Fannie Mae' (the Federal National Mortgage Association) and Freddie Mac (the Federal Home Loan Mortgage Corporation) – government-sponsored enterprises that buy up home mortgage loans from primary lenders – found themselves unable to access liquidity in the markets and so had to accept the protection of the federal government.

On 15 September, Lehman Brothers, a large investment bank which had suffered heavy losses, filed for Chapter 11 bankruptcy. Over a weekend of meetings in Manhattan, Treasury Secretary Hank Paulson made it clear that Lehman would not be rescued with federal funds. With $54bn of mortgage-backed securities on its books, Lehman Brothers was unable to attract a buyer.[12] Lehman's demise was especially unnerving, because it undermined the comfortable assumption that certain investment houses were too big for the Treasury and Federal Reserve to let fail.[13] By this point it was clear that the credit crisis was systemic, and that it had the potential to become catastrophic. Indeed, there was a moment in September 2008 when US Treasury and Federal Reserve officials thought they were looking at a financial apocalypse: not just credit crunch, but a generalised run on the country's banks.

This worst case was averted. But the steep, sustained and stomach-wrenching unwinding of a heavily leveraged economy continued into a deep recession and still-born recovery. At the start of 2012, nearly one in ten American workers was officially unemployed. And while those numbers were edging downward to the great relief of the Obama administration, they hid a wider and more persistent problem; official unemployment statistics do not include workers who no longer qualify for benefits or who have given up looking for work. Hence, the actual rate of unemployment or underemployment was closer to 16%.[14]

Austerity politics

It was obvious from the start that the main hope for avoiding a repeat of the Great Depression was to avoid the political and policy blunders that were committed by the leaders of the major economic powers in the late 1920s and 1930s. This required two things above all: the government had to come up with some means to ensure that the banks remain liquid long enough to recover from their losses and restore their capital buffers; and it needed to counteract the collapse of consumer spending and business investment. What was not clear was how to achieve these two objectives given the unique economic circumstances and the contentious political environment. Policymakers had little choice but to experiment their way through the more unique aspects of the crisis, including the scope of interdependence between banks within and across national boundaries and the complexity of their financial dealings. Often they had no clear idea how best to proceed and so were forced to muddle through with greater or lesser effectiveness.[15]

The onset and deepening of the crisis coincided with the election and inauguration of the new president, and it seemed at first that both the outgoing Bush administration and incoming Obama administration were determined and able to do what was necessary. The 'Geithner plan' put forward by Treasury Secretary Timothy Geithner, announced on 23 March 2009, expanded and repackaged the troubled asset relief programme (TARP), the Bush administration's bank bailout, establishing a public–private investment programme involving $70–$100bn of new capital from the bailout funds, leveraged to buy up to $1 trillion of toxic assets from banks.[16] The second prong of the Obama administration's response was a stimulus package: $787bn in tax cuts, public infrastructure investment and aid to the states – whose dire fiscal situation and inability to borrow threatened a pro-cyclical contraction in spending at just the time when the opposite was required. Meanwhile, Britain's Labour government also engineered large bank bailouts and kept spending high as counter-cyclical medicine for a sick economy. China joined in massive fiscal stimulus via an impressive infrastructure investment programme.

The consensus view among economists is that these stimulus measures were necessary and successful in averting a much greater slowdown in economic activity.[17] But they were not adequate to the scale of the slump. The Obama administration underestimated the extent of rising unemployment and anyway felt it had to size its stimulus package to political realities. This meant staying well below a trillion dollars at a time when at least $1.5 trillion was needed to fill the hole in demand.[18] In effect, $787bn barely compensated for the automatic contraction in spending by state and local governments which could not run deficits and which experienced a huge loss in tax revenues because of the recession.[19] And with interest rates already approaching zero, there was only limited scope for monetary policy to add to the stimulus; the Federal Reserve could engage in 'quantitative easing' by purchasing financial assets and so make money more available, but it could not make money any cheaper to borrow.

Obama did not get a second chance. The new practice of threatening filibusters routinely in the Senate meant that legislation now required a supermajority of 60 votes. Meanwhile, the November 2010 midterm elections switched control over the House of Representatives to the Republican Party once the 112th Congress took the floor in 2011. The Republican leadership, which had energetically and consciously engaged in cutting taxes during the George W. Bush administration, while asserting that these cuts would stimulate the economy, turned with a vengeance against government spending as a measure of counter-cyclical demand management. In practice, to be sure, the Republican opposition was not really directed at deficits, since the insistence on low tax rates effectively guaranteed that the deficits would continue. In American conservative discourse, however, 'deficits' are not really discussed as the difference between revenue and spending. Rather, deficits are portrayed as a stand-in for government spending, which – aside from military spending – is considered bad for the economy and threatening to liberty.[20]

It is true, of course, that the Western democracies are now facing huge mountains of debt, enlarged by bank bailouts and fallen tax revenues. The case could be made that a tipping point of collapsing confidence in government bonds might be reached at some unknowable point in the near future unless governments reassert control over spending.[21] However, public debt and national output are linked through the complex relationship between taxes and spending on the one hand, and economic activity on the other hand. When governments cut spending or raise taxes to reduce the debt burden, they run the risk of slowing down the economy and so reducing tax revenues while increasing expenses on unemployment benefits, and so forth. This risk is particularly acute when the economy is already suffering. Brad DeLong and Lawrence Summers have published research indicating that government spending cuts under such circumstances can make the debt situation worse and not better.[22]

The Republican response is to emphasise the importance of business confidence. They claim that the promise of a lower debt burden achieved through austerity today will make business more likely to invest in the future. While rising debt and deficits raise several potential macroeconomic problems, the Republican critique focuses overwhelmingly on the issue of tax. The argument has a certain logic behind it. When firms look at ever-mounting public debts, they can only imagine that taxes will have to rise. What they cannot imagine is when that will happen or how much it will cost them. Hence, so the argument runs, firms should regard government borrowing as a source of uncertainty and, faced with high levels of uncertainty, they may decide to postpone investments until they feel more confidence in their business models because the situation is easier to understand. The problem with this logic is that many other factors have an influence on business confidence than possible future changes in the tax code. Of course firms lobbying against the expiry of the Bush tax cuts will tend to stress the importance of this one variable, but the actual models they use in making investment decisions include many others. The same is true in economic analysis, which often omits possible changes in the tax code from the list of potential causes of investment. Hence evidence in support of the proposition that austerity promotes investment and therefore higher levels of economic activity in the short-to-medium term is scant.

Austerity is, however, a policy preference that American Republicans have shared with much of Europe. Continental Europeans, led by Germany's Chancellor Angela Merkel, consistently resisted Keynesian arguments for deficit spending to counteract the drop in consumption and investment. From the outset, they argued that Europe's welfare states already enacted considerable fiscal stimulus, including the 'automatic stabiliser' effects of more generous transfer mechanisms to continue paying the unemployed (which had the added political–psychological effect, initially at least, of making the crisis feel like less of an emergency than in the United States). If anything, Europe's leaders worried that in some of their welfare states, this automatic spending was unaffordable. Not all continental Europeans were determined to embrace austerity, but few were willing to stand up to the German chancellor on the issue, particularly once she was backed into a corner by an angry public, a collapsing coalition partner and a sceptical constitutional court. (Hence French President Nicolas Sarkozy periodically raised the promise of fiscal stimulus only to recant on the eve of one of the regular Franco-German summits.) And in May 2010, the UK joined its European partners in favouring debt-driven austerity over fiscal expansion, when the Labour government was replaced by a Conservative–Liberal Democrat coalition.

The sovereign-debt crisis that started in November 2009 appeared to confirm the Germans' worst suspicions. But the appearance was misleading. Outside Greece, the sovereign-debt crisis was not primarily a fiscal crisis. Unfortunately, the fiscal dimension came to overwhelm much of the policy debate.[23] The Greek government was the first to get into trouble, ostensibly through a combination of poor accounting, bureaucratic incompetence, tax evasion, cronyism and corruption. The Irish were not far behind, erasing the results of decades of painful fiscal consolidation measures almost overnight with a political decision to underwrite the liabilities of the country's stricken banks. Portugal came next, despite that country's best efforts to stay in the markets. Then, by the summer of 2011, the bond markets turned on Spain and Italy, countries large enough that their debt-market troubles could truly threaten Europe's monetary union.[24]

In the years-long succession of crisis measures to save the euro – large financial bailouts for Greece, Ireland and Portugal, European Central Bank purchases of sovereign debt in secondary markets, and unlimited access to low-interest, long-term lending for private banks – Germany made a number of important concessions to European solidarity. What the governing German parties would not do, however, was to abandon their conviction that immediate spending cuts by indebted governments, equating to significant constraints on Europe-wide aggregate demand, were a crucial part of resolving the crisis. Indeed, Chancellor Merkel insisted on negotiating a fiscal compact to embed austerity as a legal requirement. Economic logic aside, the requirement raised a problem of political realism. In her maiden speech as managing director of the IMF, Christine Lagarde highlighted this problem:

> Credible decisions on future consolidation – involving both revenue and expenditure – create space for policies that support growth and jobs today. At the same time, growth is necessary for fiscal credibility – after all, who will believe that commitments to cut spending can survive a lengthy stagnation with prolonged high unemployment and social dissatisfaction?[25]

This was from a section of her speech devoted to the United States, but it was prescient about Europe. As this book went to press in late spring 2012, Greek voters had backed parties of the extreme right and left committed to tearing up the austerity promises. These parties could not form a government, setting Greece up for new elections and continued uncertainty that would reverberate through the eurozone. In France, meanwhile, voters chose a more moderate option, replacing Sarkozy as president with the Socialist candidate François Hollande. But Hollande too had campaigned on the promise to renegotiate the austerity agreement.

The charge frequently levelled against critics of austerity is that we imagine there to be easy solutions to these dilemmas. We do not. It is obvious that the countries facing sovereign debt crises cannot, on their own accord, simply spend their way out of trouble while remaining locked in the euro. Their cost of borrowing would indeed become unbearable. But the price of restoring European growth can only be paid by those who are capable of paying it. This probably means some mutualisation of debt through the institution of eurobonds, and, as Martin Wolf has prescribed, 'a buoyant eurozone economy and higher wage growth and inflation in core economies than in the enfeebled periphery'.[26] By core economies he means, first and foremost, Germany's. Accepting both responsibility for other countries' debt and the necessity of higher inflation would indeed be a burden. It may be the only way to save the euro. But it does, admittedly, raise the similar problem of political realism.

Balance and imbalance

Of course, the long-term debt problem of advanced industrial countries does need to be fixed. The question is one of priority. Focusing exclusively on debt problems at a time of persistently high unemployment is akin to shoring up the foundations of a burning house.

The most urgent problem facing the world right now is the weakness of the most advanced industrial economies. Both the United States and the countries of Europe need to grow to escape from their debts. Only then should they work to address the structural origins of the crisis. Some of the problems are mechanical and derive from the integration of international financial markets; others are conceptual and can be found in the models and assumptions used to anticipate economic performance. Assuming that the United States can climb out of its stagnation, Americans will need to reconsider the origins of the catastrophe to avoid repeating it.[27]

The first step is to recognise that government indebtedness is the symptom of the economic turmoil and not the cause. The different countries involved in the crisis are now heavily indebted, but they are indebted because of their involvement in the crisis, and not the other way around. In the United States, although it is true that the George W. Bush administration racked up significant debts through unfunded tax cuts and high military spending, these public debts did not directly cause bubbles to form in different parts of the US housing market, they did not result in consumers borrowing several times their household income and they did not encourage banks to borrow many more times their available capital.

By contrast, bank bailouts did grow the public debt in a very direct and immediate sense. So did the slowdown in consumer spending as households began to tighten their belts, albeit more indirectly, and so did the collapse in house prices and the dramatic rise in repossessions and defaults. Once the US economy had ground to a halt, the government stepped in to make up some of the difference. This stimulus was necessary; it was also expensive (see Figure 3, 'US federal debt as a percentage of GDP', page 203).

The origins of the crisis lie in the different patterns of savings and investment across the global economy. The situation in Europe prior to the crisis offers the most intuitive illustration. The countries of northern Europe tended to save more than they invested, for simple enough reasons. North European workers were already highly productive and relatively expensive, which limited the opportunities for investment. Meanwhile, North European populations were old and ageing quickly, which created strong incentives to save. The situation in southern Europe was slightly reversed. Southern European populations were also old and ageing quickly, but the workers were relatively cheap and less productive. The south European countries could also draw on new pools of immigrant labour to work in construction or to provide household services. On balance, this meant that the opportunities for profitable investment were plentiful in southern Europe relative to the north. Hence surplus savings flowed from northern Europe to finance investments in the south even before Europeans introduced their common currency at the end of the 1990s.

A similar relationship developed between the United States and China, but the logic is different. The United States is rich and technologically advanced. US workers are expensive relative to their Chinese counterparts. All things being equal, the intuitive guess would be that China should have lower savings and offer better prospects for investment. However, the opposite turns out to have been the case. There are significant opportunities for profitable investment in China, but these are complicated by political interference and the weakness of the rule of law. More importantly, the Chinese government creates barriers to the free movement of capital, the domestic banking system is inefficient, and the country's central bank and sovereign wealth fund actively shift domestic savings abroad through the accumulation of foreign-exchange reserves and more active forms of asset portfolio management. As a consequence, China saves far more than it invests.

The United States' situation is counter-intuitive as well. The US economy saves little and invests a lot. This pattern can be explained in many ways, ranging from the voracious appetite of American consumers with easy credit access, to the dynamism of American innovation and entrepreneurship and the stability of the United States as a safe haven offering both physical security against foreign aggressors and a predictable rule of law. Some, like the Kennedy School's Riccardo Hausmann, have even gone so far as to suggest that Americans have a hidden talent for reaping profits from investments both at home and abroad – and that this unaccounted 'dark matter' actually offsets much of the United States' apparent level of foreign borrowing.[28]

Whatever the explanation, the fact is that savings and investment were hugely out of balance in China and in the United States. And the more the two countries interacted, the more this imbalance between savings and investment could accumulate. The Chinese acquired enormous foreign-exchange reserves and dollar-denominated assets; the United States accumulated an ever deeper pool of toxic mortgage-backed securities used to finance an ever-expanding real estate market bubble. Something similar happened within Europe. The north Europeans collected southern European sovereign-debt instruments; the southern Europeans expanded into ever more risky investments. Neither situation could go on forever, and so (as Stein's Law would predict) they stopped.[29] The economic and financial crises revealed that the huge imbalances accumulated across countries were unsustainable. Instead of a self-correcting global market centred on a dynamic US economy, the world experienced a catastrophic market failure with the United States at its epicentre. As this crisis spread to Europe, it presented an existential threat to the euro and perhaps even the European Union itself.

Power shift?

This ongoing threat to Europe, combined with the fact that an economically weakened United States remains heavily indebted to China, inspires frequent predictions that the international system will undergo rapid redistributions of global wealth and power. Such predictions are hardly new. For more than a generation there have been expectations of strategic and economic power shifts from the Euro-Atlantic arena towards Asia-Pacific in general and China in particular. Often these predictions glossed over the reality that China, if and when it surpassed the United States in terms of total output, would remain, per capita, a poor country with huge political challenges and an ageing population posing demographic challenges of equal magnitude to Europe's and considerably worse than the United States'. Still, the Great Recession of 2008–09 and ongoing economic and financial crises in the United States and Europe have thrown the question of respective geopolitical weights into sharper perspective. China and other Asia-Pacific nations appear to have weathered the economic crisis rather well. The United States and Europe, by contrast, remain mired in it.

Certainly, the US share of military and economic aggregates is likely to shrink in comparison with the increasing shares claimed by China, India, Brazil and other rising powers. This is a form of American decline, but we need to be precise in how we understand the term. Relative decline is both inevitable and benign insofar as it is the consequence of a strategy that America has pursued since the Second World War: helping other countries to become richer and more successful. The United States could, in theory, pursue a goal of trying to keep China mired in poverty, but it is hard to imagine what a strategy for pursuing that goal would look like; it would appear on its face to be immoral, and the consequences could be dangerous. Relative American decline is a benign future compared to plausible alternatives, but it does pose a serious strategic challenge, because it suggests that, over the long term, American hegemony will become more difficult to sustain.[30]

Americans could more logically worry about actual degradation of economic well-being, future capabilities and national morale – what Calleo has called 'morbid decline'. Calleo has long argued that this condition can be self-inflicted in large measure through unsustainable efforts to maintain global hegemony. It is in these terms that he has analysed the history of America's global role. America assumed an extraordinary burden after 1945 in financing the world's – especially Europe's – post-war economic recovery, and in extending its military protection against Soviet threats. This was not pure altruism, of course, but the fact that economic recovery and strategic stability were manifestly in the American interest did not diminish the generosity of the US post-war project. American relative decline started at about the same time, insofar as the United States emerged from the Second World War with roughly half of global GDP, and that share started to decline almost immediately. As the Cold War matured, and Japan, Germany and other European states prospered, America's central role in the international economy declined as well. Nevertheless, the centrality of the United States in the design of post-war institutions remained undiminished and the growing gap between the relative size and capacity of the US economy and its institutional obligations created strain for the international system as a whole.

The Bretton Woods system is a good illustration of this dynamic. The US role in the Bretton Woods arrangement carried at least two significant long-term implications for the world economy that continued well after the collapse of the system of fixed-but-adjustable exchanges. To begin with, the US dollar remains the principal reserve currency and safe haven. As a consequence, the US government can borrow at relatively low rates of interest from the rest of the world almost under any circumstances; when S&P downgraded America's coveted triple-A credit rating in August 2011, the yield on US treasury certificates actually declined.[31] This is the essence of what then French Finance Minister Valéry Giscard D'Estaing famously called America's 'exorbitant privilege'.[32]

The extraordinary capacity of the US government to borrow from the rest of the world is a problem for the global system because it has allowed Washington to ignore fundamental strategic choices and limits. Paul Kennedy was among the many to argue that the United States has consistently spent more on defence than was prudent.[33] The role of the dollar as safe-haven is also a problem, because it encourages excess liquidity growth in the United States, particularly when other parts of the world run into difficulties. This is what happened in the aftermath of the Asian financial crisis at the end of the 1990s.

Another concern is that the US dollar is the numerator or reference point for the exchange-rate policies of other countries. The most obvious example today is China, but the Asian giant is hardly the first to be in that situation. The West European countries – principally Germany – accumulated large reserves of dollar-denominated assets during the 1960s when the dollar lay at the centre of the Bretton Woods system. At the time, such dollar reserves were viewed both as a symptom of European efforts to maintain a competitive exchange rate and as an implicit subsidy for US leadership of the Western alliance – what Calleo has compared to a kind of 'imperial tax' levied by the United States on its allies.[34] The contrast with current debates about China is a reflection of the different security environment. China subsidises American consumers; the Europeans subsidised the US military (and so by extension the defence of the West).

The Cold War environment also explains European acquiescence to the implicit subsidy for the US government. Enjoying American military protection while their own defence budgets remained modest, the Europeans were able to enjoy economic growth and to finance generous welfare states, and hence they were reluctant to complain too loudly. Like China today, the Europeans also benefited from access to US consumers. Yet the dollar balances had inflationary consequences for countries such as France, where inflation was becoming an acute and endemic problem in the 1960s. For de Gaulle, taking tutelage from the economist Jacques Rueff, the whole system had become 'abusive and dangerous'. Yet, however much they might have grumbled, there was during the Cold War an enduring reason for European leaders to accept the situation. 'All things considered,' as

Calleo has noted, 'the costs of accumulating the exported dollars was a cheap price for America's protection, and awkward to refuse.'[35] The Chinese face a similar predicament. They may resent the criticism periodically emanating from the US Congress and they may grow frustrated with what they see as the excesses of the US economy, but they are in no position to cut themselves off from US consumer markets.[36]

Such relationships are unlikely to prove stable over the long run and have resulted in periodic crises and grievances throughout the post-war era and into the post-Cold War. The closure of the 'gold window' by the Nixon administration in the early 1970s is one example; the onset of the global economic and financial crisis in 2008 is another. In both cases, it was tensions within the United States, and not between the United States and its economic partners, that proved decisive.[37]

Drawing on Calleo's work, Skidelsky traced these linkages in a 2009 speech to the IISS annual Global Strategic Review. He noted that the American privilege of *seignorage* had somehow survived past the 1990s as East Asian economies, China in particular, hoarded vast dollar reserves. One could engage in a chicken-or-egg argument about whether Chinese over-saving or American over-consumption was the principal driver, but one consequence was cheap credit in the United States inflating first the 'dotcom' bubble of the 1990s and then the housing bubble of the following decade. It is a mistake, possibly, to burden economic analysis with too much moral baggage, for the idea that the system '"has enabled the Americans to live beyond their means" is too vague to be useful'. One needs to ask, as Skidelsky does:

which Americans? Certainly many middle- and low-income American households have been given access to credit beyond their means. But secondly, the American–Chinese symbiosis has been excellent for US business profits. American businessmen have been complicit in Chinese 'super-competitiveness' by offshoring well-paid manufacturing jobs to China in order to cut costs. The decline in US manufacturing and growth in non-tradable services, and the financial operations which secured this re-structuring, have enabled financiers and businessmen to earn huge profits which should have been shared with their workers. Morally, the financial community has been living well beyond its means. But, perhaps above all the American current account deficit has enabled the US government to live beyond its means, by getting other countries to finance its imperial pretensions.[38]

The link to America's strategic role is convincing, according to Skidelsky, if one is 'clear about the causal mechanisms by which "surplus Chinese saving" became "excessive American spending". Evidently, the Americans didn't directly spend Chinese savings.' Instead, the dollars paid to Chinese exporters were lent to and used by the Chinese central bank to purchase US Treasury bills. This operation had the dual effect of 'sterilising' China's dollar inflow – thus keeping the renminbi's exchange-rate low – and allowing the US government to borrow vast sums without 'crowding out' lending and spending at home. So it was that 'Chinese savings made it possible for the US consumer to go on a spending spree. This explanation brings out the role of the US fiscal deficit in precipitating the financial meltdown.'[39]

It could be argued, of course, that these systemic imbalances were better than any alternative. One such argument held that, in the face of a massive East Asian propensity to save, American spending staved off global deflation: the United States served in this period as 'borrower and spender of last resort', as Martin Wolf has put it.[40] But, for the imbalances to be sustainable, the system somehow needed to recycle Chinese savings into productive US investments, rather than a manic bidding up of house prices. A second argument, discussed in chapter 2, would posit expansive credit as preferable to letting the 9/11 attacks cause a 'fear-induced recession'.

More was financed, however, than just a recovery from panic. Skidelsky has suggested that American conservatives ignored the fiscal side of Bush-era easy money 'no doubt because they believed the deficits were incurred in the worthy cause of the "war on terror."'[41] Bill Emmott, the former editor of *The Economist*, has gone further. Reflecting on the tenth anniversary of the 11 September attacks, Emmott argued that the most devastating consequence has been the global economic crisis that still afflicts us. Like Skidelsky, Emmott believes that the wars bin Laden provoked were a direct cause of the crash – both in the direct costs they incurred and in the wider mindset they inspired. '[T]hink of the psychology,' Emmott writes:

> If Mr Greenspan was so ideologically determined to keep his hands off the markets, why did he raise rates six times to burst the dotcom bubble in 1999?

Why after 2001, by contrast, did he keep pumping in credit to housing and banks, even as another bubble formed? Why did fiscal policy under the presidency of George W. Bush, a supposed conservative (compassionate or otherwise) also turn expansionary, with spending soaring and taxes cut? Why, in the run-up to the 2005 election did Tony Blair and Mr Brown keep up their spending splurge on health and education? The answer is simple. There was a war on, or rather two wars, not even counting the vague one on terror. At such times the inclination to risk an economic slowdown or new recession diminishes: after 9/11, President Bush said that Americans should do the patriotic thing and go out spending again.[42]

This argument relies on some hypothetical assumptions. Yet Emmott is clearly onto an important insight regarding the psychology of the American political class in relation to America's world role. That class is unlikely to concede that the role of world policeman requires an explicit trade-off against Americans' living standards. The Johnson administration was not willing to propose such a trade-off to pay for the Vietnam War, and the George W. Bush administration was unwilling to do so regarding Iraq. Note, moreover, that the problem is not confined to a special category of 'unnecessary wars', under which the present authors would file both Iraq and Vietnam. Using the same criteria, the 1991 war to reverse Iraq's invasion of Kuwait was, in our view, both justified and necessary, and it is easy to imagine future necessary wars that are practically required by America's global security role – for example, a war on the Korean Peninsula caused by the belligerent regime in Pyongyang. Korea is, in fact, an excellent example, because it was the battleground of America's first post-war police action. The Second World War that preceded it was considered an existential contest, for which it was natural to expect Americans to mobilise every sinew of state, society and economy. This was an emergency, however, lasting for the United States less than four years. By contrast, a permanent war footing (spending half the world's defence dollars can hardly be seen as anything else) for the permanent position of world's policeman requires either an endless source of deficit financing, or a fundamental rethink about the nature and purposes of the American state.

CHAPTER FIVE

Power, influence and leadership

> I think it's important for all Americans to remem-
> ber, over the past ten years, since 9/11, our defence
> budget grew at an extraordinary pace. Over the
> next ten years, the growth in the defence budget
> will slow, but the fact of the matter is this: it will
> still grow, because we have global responsibilities
> that demand our leadership.
>
> Barack Obama, 5 January 2012[1]

Five years into the global economic and financial crisis and
three years into his presidency, Barack Obama initiated a
review of national security policy, in his words, 'to clarify
our strategic interests in a fast-changing world, and to guide
our defence priorities and spending over the coming decade'.
The result was a widely heralded pivot to the Pacific, a drawdown on conventional forces in favour of special-operations
units and unmanned drones, and a gradual deceleration in
the growth of military outlays.[2]

Critics complained that this change in budgeting and force posture undermined American power and they found it easy to illustrate aspects of the new defence budget proposal that they did not like. [3] They found it harder to come up with a plausible alternative and harder still to justify the status quo. Including the costs of wars in Afghanistan and Iraq, US defence spending in FY2011 exceeded $710 billion – a constant-dollar increase of almost 90% over the amount in 1998.[4] Such expenditures are clearly unsustainable and were already declining. While base outlays increased by $2.7bn between fiscal years 2010 and 2012, the cost of operations in Iraq and Afghanistan fell by $47.2bn.[5] Iraq spending fell from a high of $142.1bn in 2008 to $43.9bn in 2011; meanwhile, over the same period, the annual cost of the war in Afghanistan rose from $43.4bn to $118.6bn. The official cumulative costs of wars in Iraq, Afghanistan and other 'overseas contingency operations' between FY2001–FY2012, come to more than $1.4 trillion (a figure that does not include significant indirect costs such as future health care for permanently disabled war veterans). These war costs came on top of a base defence budget of well over half a trillion dollars per year. (For more detail on defence budgets for FY2010–FY2012 and outlay for the US' overseas contingencies, see Appendix Tables 1 and 2, on pages 199 and 202 respectively).[6]

The bitter debates over the size and shape of the federal budget between the Obama administration and the Republicans ensured that defence expenditure would be implicated in efforts to rein in the deficit. The Republican position generally was that defence spending should be exempt from cost-cutting pressures elsewhere. The Obama administration's 'defense strategic guidance' document of January 2012 implied modest restraint but continued growth. There had been some significant cuts – notably, the decision by Robert Gates, Obama's first defence secretary, to halt the F-22 stealth fighter programme, and a reduction of the army's active-duty troop level from 570,000, in 2010, to a planned 490,000. 'The Army and Marine Corps will no longer need to be sized to support large-scale stability operations,' said Leon Panetta, the new defense secretary, upon release of the guidance document. At nearly half a million, however, the army would remain larger than it was in 2001. Scenarios can no doubt be envisioned to justify such a land force. Meanwhile, in deference to the new emphasis on balancing in the Asia-Pacific, Navy forces including capacity for 11 carrier groups were to be maintained.

It would be difficult indeed to make the case that such plans constituted an evisceration of US defence capabilities. Of course, with global responsibilities and a theoretically unlimited set of conceivable military conflicts, it becomes surpassingly difficult to anchor the defence debate in any realistic notion of how much is enough. One category of measurement would invoke comparative defence statistics. Here the results are striking: in 2011 the US spent 8.2 times more on defence than its nearest competitor, China. Moreover, the top nine defence budgets after the United States include four of America's treaty allies: the UK, France, Germany and Japan; and one strategic partner, Saudi Arabia. The remaining leading defence budgets are those of India, Brazil and Russia. Put differently, US FY2011 defence spending of $739.3bn comfortably exceeded the

$486.4bn combined spending of the next nine powers, and of those nine powers, only two could be considered even remotely hostile to the United States (See Appendix, Figure 2 'Comparative defence statistics', pages 200–1).[7]

Another form of comparison is historical. As defence journalist Fred Kaplan notes, in 1985, 'at the height of President Ronald Reagan's Cold War arms build-up, the Pentagon's budget [adjusted for inflation] amounted to $575 billion', compared to an Obama defence budget of $525bn, or $671bn if the costs of war in Afghanistan and other operations are included. Kaplan continues, with some incredulity: 'In an era when we face no foes of remotely comparable military power, how could it be that we need to spend roughly as much as we spent when the Soviet Union was alive, the Cold War was heating up, the border between East and West Germany was an armed garrison, and the nuclear arms race was spiralling upward?'[8] Indeed, the graph 'DoD budget authority' on page 199 shows that America's defence spending surpassed Cold-War peaks in 2006.

There was a period during the 1990s when US defence expenditures fell dramatically. The first Gulf War and the violent breakup of Yugoslavia notwithstanding, the end of the Cold War offered a peace dividend which contributed significantly to the fiscal consolidation undertaken during the successive administrations of Bill Clinton. According to historical data from the Office of Management and Budget, the national defence cost $298bn when Clinton won the White House in 1992 and just $266 billion by the end of his first term in office. Moreover, those are nominal dollar amounts and the reduction in real outlays was much greater. The share of national defence in the total budget fell from 22% to 17% over the same period even as the share of gross domestic product (GDP) fell from 4.8% to just 3.4%. And while the nominal dollar value of defence expenditures rose by the end of the Clinton administration to back to $294bn, the share of defence in total outlays fell further to just under 16.5% and the GDP share fell to 3%. The period after 9/11 witnessed a strong reversal of this trend. By the time Barack Obama won office in 2008, the nominal value of defence outlays was $616bn, the share of government outlays was just under 21%, and the share of GDP was 4.3%.[9] If the cumulative costs of the wars in Afghanistan and Iraq were included, the difference would be even more striking.

The United States needs to cut military expenditure to strengthen its domestic economy and it needs to strengthen its domestic economy in order to provide a stable foundation for financing America's world role. Nevertheless, the imperatives of acting as a global policeman tend to trump the long-term requirements for sound economic management. The United States grows weaker by overexerting its strength. This is the crux of the dilemma for those who believe the United States must adapt to a more plural world of many great powers. The challenge for such pluralists is to anticipate not only how such a world would be organised, but also how other countries will react to these necessary adaptations by the United States.

A world without followers

Sometimes perceptions create their own realities. Even if we choose to ignore the material constraints on the exercise of US foreign policy, the simple fact that there is such intense debate about the declining influence of the United States could have important implications for the stability of the global system – a system designed by American political leaders to sustain and reinforce America's global role. Other countries will only buy into an American-centred global order if they believe that the US government is willing and able to underwrite that system, if they can have an equitable chance to pursue their own self-interest, if they believe that other powerful actors will not violate the rules of the game and so take advantage of them.[10]

The usual presumption about power is that if one country gets another to do something it otherwise would not do, or prevents it from doing something it otherwise would, the explanation can be traced to some attribute of the country doing the persuading – the strength of its army, the wealth of its economy or the hold it has over public opinion or the popular imagination. This is the spectrum of power that runs from the coercive hard to the attractive soft, covering all points in between. Countries can have many attributes in combination and they can develop new ones such as extensive social networks, dynamic markets, effective schools and creative universities. Moreover, politicians can use their national resources poorly or they can use them well; they can squander their power assets or they can be smart. The key feature in this presumption is that power is something that countries posses or can develop. Power belongs to countries by dint of their resources and, so long as we can take the structure of relations between countries for granted, the distribution of resources should offer a good guide as to how conflicts between countries will work out.[11]

Much of the current speculation about the future is that power will follow the growth in relative wealth and population.[12] The gist of the argument is that current trends will not lead to a total eclipse of the United States, but they will result in its relative decline. And the preliminary evidence in terms of trade, investment and short-term capital flows suggests that the argument has merit, at least in broad terms. The rise of Germany within Europe and Europe within the Atlantic Alliance has altered the incentives for Europeans to accept American hegemony. The rise of China and India outside the Western system – and of Turkey and Brazil as middle-ranking powers – has altered the incentives to accept the rules, norms and conventions of a Western-dominated world (see Appendix: Figure 4 'Real historical gross domestic product for selected countries', page 203).

These trends are well established in the writings of such commentators as Thomas Friedman and Fareed Zakaria.[13] However, the conclusion they draw is different from what is suggested here. Power has not shifted from West to East (or, in Zakaria's wording, from the West to the Rest); rather, power has diminished as coordination both within and between groups has faltered. The negotiation of the Uruguay Round of the General Agreement on Tariffs and Trade (1986–94) became very difficult; the Doha Development Round of talks within the WTO, which began in 2001, are now moribund. Meanwhile, efforts to create parallel forms of coordination or 'go it alone' strategies have fractured the original system. Thus the original Bretton Woods currency arrangement evolved into the current monetary disorder, and a 'spaghetti bowl' of bilateral trade agreements is inundating the old multilateral trading system.[14]

What such speculation does not reveal is how a new global order will emerge from the present crisis. In a context where the structure of relationships between countries cannot be taken for granted, a new set of presumptions about the nature of power comes into play. Resources still matter, but relationships matter as much or more. When Richard Cooper set out his analysis of *The Economics of Interdependence* in the late 1960s, he explained how even the government responsible for managing the world's largest economy could only achieve its policy objectives by taking the actions of its major partners into account. Hence national policymakers faced a choice: either they could learn to work together with their counterparts in other countries, or they would have to scale back on their country's relations with the world economy as a whole.[15]

The logic of interdependence is becoming stronger. George W. Bush was able to come into office at the turn of the century with a strong commitment to American unilateralism. He could turn his back on the Kyoto Protocol for the reduction of greenhouse gas emissions, the Anti-Ballistic Missile accords, and the International Criminal Court (ICC), without much concern for how foreign reactions to his positions would impact on the effectiveness of US policy. Barack Obama could not afford the same luxury eight years later. He had to worry about how other countries would react to American efforts to shore up the big US banks, just as he had to recognise that international cooperation would enhance the effectiveness of US economic policy.

This problem of interdependence has become a pressing concern in other areas as well – from energy security to environmental protection, and from international terrorism to organised crime to piracy. No matter how much in terms of resources the United States is willing to throw at any of these problems, what is obvious is that no solution will be forthcoming unless other state actors come along. Moreover, their essential cooperation cannot be compelled if it is to be meaningful – or at least any more meaningful than Pakistan's efforts to stop the Taliban.

Meanwhile, the United States has to be on the lookout for countries or other actors who seek to exploit any vulnerabilities that present themselves. The pirates in the Indian Ocean have built their business model on the recognition that it is easier for shipping magnates to pay the occasional ransom than to reroute freight traffic around the Horn of Africa. As a result, they not only pursued their trade with impunity but may also have come to regard it as accepted practice – which partly explains why the pirates responded so angrily to the forceful liberation by US Navy SEALs of Captain Richard Phillips in April 2009.

Whereas the pirates exploit state vulnerability, the North Koreans and Iranians engage in varying degrees of blackmail, breaking the rules to take advantage of the uncertainty they create. The North Korean case is the most acute. By timing their missile test to coincide with a G20 summit, they forced the Obama administration to focus its attention on their concerns. The Iranian case is more subtle. They do not need to demonstrate such an obvious threat in order to raise doubts and attract attention.

Here it is useful to return to the relative importance of resource distribution and collective action. Individuals can be weak or powerful; groups can be weak or powerful as well. The difference between strength and weakness is partly a function of the distribution of resources, but it is also a matter of coordination. It is intuitively obvious that governments with significant resources at their disposal usually run powerful countries. Alliances with significant resources are usually powerful as well.

All things being equal, better coordinated groups are more powerful – meaning they are better able to influence their environments, including the actions of both those within the group and those outside.[16] The obvious question is how to improve coordination within a group. Institutions – rules, norms, conventions – offer one set of solutions, but their effectiveness depends on a mix of incentives and enforcement, which can depend, in turn, on the effectiveness of leadership. An effective leader can create incentives to encourage others to adopt and abide by the rules of the game; a leader can also step in to enforce the rules for those who are less compliant.

When coordination breaks down

Whatever the objective merits of the United States as a world actor or global policeman, if other major actors lack confidence in America's ability to maintain open markets, if they believe that the global economic system is rigged against them, if they perceive other actors such as China or Germany to be taking advantage of the system, and if they lose confidence in the dollar as the ultimate vehicle for international payments, then they may begin to withdraw their support from an American-centred world order.

This diagnosis is shared by members of Barack Obama's administration, and was reflected in their 2010 National Security Strategy. The document repeated many elements from the national security strategies produced by the Bush administration in 2002 and 2006, as those responsible for drafting the new version were quick to acknowledge.[17] Nevertheless, the 2010 National Security Strategy was unlike its predecessors in placing so much emphasis on rebuilding the economic foundations of American power. This emphasis is hardly surprising, given the context within which the strategy was drafted. It emerged at the end of the worst economic downturn since the Great Depression of the 1930s. As a consequence, it placed America's economic weakness up front:

> Our approach begins with a commitment to build a stronger foundation for American leadership, because what takes place within our borders will determine our strength and influence beyond them ... At the center of our efforts is a commitment to renew our economy, which serves as the wellspring of American power.

The United States' economy must be secure, resilient, disciplined and competitive 'in order to sustain America's ability to lead in a world where economic power and individual opportunity are more diffuse'. To be successful, however, America's performance must also be consistent with American values.

> Finally, the work to build a stronger foundation for our leadership within our borders recognises that the most effective way for the United States of America to promote our values is to live them ... America has always been a beacon to the peoples of the world when we ensure that the light of America's example burns bright.[18]

The programme set out in the document contains a mixture of initiatives to promote domestic education, innovation and investment – particularly in the energy domain. In turn, these efforts are embedded in a systematic reform of the global economic system to make it more representative, more stable and more equitable. For those who are familiar with the pluralist or declinist argument, this is a coherent strategy for action. What remains to be seen is whether the United States has the strength to drive that agenda.

Throughout his first administration, President Obama has been looking for friends and allies to help shoulder the burden. That is why the 2010 National Security Strategy refers to the importance of maintaining strong alliances and why it insists that: 'Our relationship with our European allies remains the cornerstone for US engagement with the world, and a catalyst for international action.'[19] The implication is that other countries will have to continue to embrace American leadership, not just in Europe but elsewhere as well. US Deputy Secretary of State James Steinberg made the point succinctly when he argued at the International Institute for Strategic Studies Global Strategic Review in September 2010 that: 'The decision to reinvigorate global cooperation is not ours alone, but we can play a powerful and important role in shaping that decision for other countries.' The possibility left open is that other countries may decide not to follow where the United States tries to lead.

The problem is that the United States can no longer afford to offer many incentives. Global macroeconomic imbalances have become unsustainable insofar as America is no longer able to underwrite the global economic system as consumer of last resort[20] (see Appendix, Figure 3, 'US federal debt as a percentage of GDP', Figure 5, 'US trade in goods and services: balance of payments basis' and Figure 6 'US reserve assets', pages 203–4). Hence, the United States is asking countries like Germany, Japan and China to change the export-led growth formulas that made it possible for them to thrive under American hegemony. That is a hard sell. It is made all the harder by the prospect that divided government will prevent the US from making other concessions that could ease the pain.

The United States will also have difficulty finding followers because other countries are less willing to identify with the international system as a collection of rules and institutions. This is a subtly different point because it has less to do with incentives, or how countries benefit from the system; instead the focus is on where the system does them harm. Germany is not part of the group of five permanent members of the UN Security Council; China has only as many votes in the IMF as Belgium and the Netherlands. Every country can see problems with the system of global institutions and each has its own view as to how the system should be reformed, leading to wrangles about IMF directorships and voting weights as well as reform of the UN Security Council. In such disputes, the Obama bounce in global public opinion polling does not make much difference. Countries may like the United States and admire its leadership, but that says very little about how they want to interact with one another even if they believe that the US should continue to run the show.

What is lacking in 2012 is any clear vision of how to reconcile the competing ambitions of rising and declining powers in a manner that will promote a stable and effective pattern of international cooperation in the future. There is a lot of talk of promoting the Group of 20 (G20) in lieu of the Group of 8 (G8), reforming the United Nations Security Council, and redesigning the voting rules for the International Monetary Fund, but there is little sense of how this somehow constitutes a coherent global framework. Indeed, with the exception of the G20 effectively replacing the G8, it is hard to see how these other changes can come about. Most of the existing global institutions – and the UN Security Council in particular – are hostage to the vested interests of the key actors who benefit from existing arrangements. As a result, they are even harder to reform than they are to do without. Of course international institutions are hardly unique in this regard and domestic institutions are difficult to reform as well. The fact that the problem is a general one, however, only makes the challenge of finding a solution all the harder.[21]

A related challenge for American diplomats as they try to play some kind of central role is that the problems they must face are so complicated and the consequences are so uncertain that it is hard to find consensus on what should be done. For example, the Obama administration is trying to tell the Germans, the Japanese and, particularly, the Chinese that the United States can no longer act as the consumer of last resort and that they will have to start investing in themselves and relying on domestic demand to stimulate output. And while it has made considerable headway in terms of changing the emphasis in the debate, none of the current-account surplus countries is willing to concede the argument. On the contrary, they are telling the United States that it is America's obligation to reform. The G20 has clearly reached an impasse on this issue – both globally and within Europe itself. It is impossible to see how to avoid a repeat of the global financial crisis if this problem of macroeconomic imbalances is not resolved.[22]

Other countries of the world are no less constrained than the United States itself. If anything, their situation may be even more problematic. Consider a simple illustration. One of the most pressing constraints on US government finances lies in the predicted rise in the percentage of Americans who are aged 60 and over, from 18 to 27% during the next four decades. In China, the elderly share of the population will go from 12 to 31%, and China is not even the worst case. South Korea will see it share of over-60s go from 15 to 41% of the total population. This peak is only slightly higher than we expect to see in Western Europe, although the starting point is much lower and so the change is correspondingly greater.[23] For India, the problem is the reverse. The population is young and expanding rapidly. Hence the world's largest democracy must struggle mightily to create enough employment to keep an already large population living in poverty from expanding even further.

These emerging-market and middle-income countries have only a short window in which to exercise anything global influence before they have to face dramatic challenges at home. This means they are not only unlikely to lead; they may be unable to follow as well. The conclusion is straightforward: the US needs cooperation now more than ever, but it is more difficult to find a willing group of followers to help.

Frustration and hubris

There is no ready alternative to American leadership and there is no obvious support for American leadership either. Some country must set the agenda and forge cooperation if all are to benefit from the power of collective action.

The United States' continued ambition to fill this role has much to do with the American political temperament and the underlying consensus in the United States on the indispensability of American power.[24] This was articulated clearly during the 2004 US presidential elections. In the first of three presidential debates, the Democratic candidate, John Kerry, led off with the following conviction: 'I believe President Bush and I both love our country equally. But we just have a different set of convictions about how you make America safe. I believe America is safest and strongest when we are leading the world and we are leading strong alliances.' This conviction was uncontroversial in the debate. Instead, the candidates sparred over who had the best formula for exercising such leadership. Kerry insisted that much hinged on

American credibility and the president's ability to pass 'the global test where your countrymen, your people understand fully why you're doing what you're doing and you can prove to the world that you did it for legitimate reasons.' The Republican incumbent, George W. Bush, insisted that leadership emanates from the strength of American values and the constancy of American commitments, because 'if America shows uncertainty or weakness in this decade, the world will drift toward tragedy'.[25]

This debate over the nature of American leadership became one of the defining moments of the 2004 campaign. The Bush campaign ridiculed Kerry for his suggestion of a 'global test' and cemented the importance of projecting American values and promoting American interests through a firm commitment to leadership abroad. Four years later, Democratic candidate and then President Barack Obama pulled the style of American leadership back in a more cooperative direction. Nevertheless, whether the administration is led by a Republican or a Democrat, the assumption that the United States should play a leading role in the world goes unchallenged.

This is why outgoing Defense Secretary Robert Gates's critique of NATO in his 10 June 2011 speech is so significant.[26] He warned:

> The blunt reality is that there will be dwindling appetite and patience in the US Congress – and in the American body politic writ large – to expend increasingly precious funds on behalf of nations that are apparently unwilling to devote the neces-

sary resources or make the necessary changes to be serious and capable partners in their own defense. Nations apparently willing and eager for American taxpayers to assume the growing security burden left by reductions in European defense budgets. Indeed, if current trends in the decline of European defense capabilities are not halted and reversed, future U.S. political leaders – those for whom the Cold War was not the formative experience that it was for me – may not consider the return on America's investment in NATO worth the cost.

US defence secretaries have always complained about burden-sharing within the alliance. As Gates himself admits, there is little new to say on that front. What is new is more implicit than explicit. The Obama administration has a lot staked on how well Europeans demonstrate the capacity to support and even share in America's leadership role. This is sure to sound strange to the Europeans themselves. Why should they be held responsible for the success or failure of the Obama administration's engagement with the outside world? Yet, if Europeans prefer this new style of American global leadership to the more unilateral alternative, then the answer to that question is self-evident. The effectiveness of any leader is a function of the efforts of those who follow. And a leader without followers has little choice but to go it alone.

Realist Dilemmas

'[T]he United States must decide which of the two sides of its national character is to predominate – the humanism of Lincoln or the arrogance of those who would make America the world's policeman.' It was understandable that J. William Fulbright, writing in 1966, appealed to the authority of Lincoln, but also a little odd, since Lincoln's presidency constituted an epic failure of realist restraint. He wanted to avoid war, and would have accepted painful moral compromise to do so. But war came nonetheless, and Lincoln prosecuted it with fierceness and, ultimately, a kind of moral absoluteness. In the process he consolidated and, in large part, created a great and crusading world power.

Today, the president does not face anything like the excruciating choices handed to Lincoln. He has, however, undertaken to maintain the United States as the leading global power and (though Obama would not use this expression) benign world policeman, while avoiding the moral arrogance and strategic over-commitment that would corrode international prestige and domestic well-being. The administration's pursuit of these goals has not entailed any radical break with the traditions of post-war American foreign policy. On the contrary, its efforts have remained well within the mainstream of foreign-policy realism as practised, in various respects, by administrations as diverse as those headed by Dwight D. Eisenhower, John F. Kennedy, Lyndon B. Johnson, Richard Nixon, Jimmy Carter, Ronald Reagan, George H.W. Bush and Bill Clinton. Not all of these presidents are remembered as realists, of course, but they and others have had conscious moments of strategic restraint when they made clear decisions to resist costly entanglements or adventures. Obama came into office at a time of acute consciousness of American overstretch, and he seemed temperamentally and intellectually well suited to practise a foreign policy of restraint. He has done so, however, following the templates that others have moulded.

Are these templates adequate to provide the time and space for America to achieve an economic and political restoration? It is hard to say. One problem is that American strategic and moral commitments have tended to ratchet up over time. While it is true that the United States was locked for most of the post-war period into massive global confrontation with a superpower adversary, that confrontation also tended to focus and limit American efforts and expectations in certain ways. Hence, America under the Nixon administration could be relatively indifferent to massacres in East Pakistan or Indonesia, while the Carter and Reagan administrations, in continuing the opening to China, gave indirect aid to the remnants of Cambodia's genocidal Khmer Rouge.

The Reagan administration, to avoid a more direct American confrontation with Iran, tacitly aligned with the regime of Saddam Hussein, even while it was using chemical weapons against civilians. Such policies followed certain strategic logic, but they would be far more difficult to pull off today.

The ratcheting up of moral concerns has also complicated American diplomacy, which is an indispensable art for avoiding unnecessary conflict and sustaining American power. Deng Xiaoping had a point when he lamented, in a conversation with Henry Kissinger that, whereas Kissinger and Nixon had pursued their opening to China without regard to the ongoing and savage Cultural Revolution, the Tiananmen Square massacre, though of lower body count, somehow posed a greater obstacle to Sino-American relations:

> At the time that you and President Nixon decided to re-establish relations with China, China was not only striving for socialism but also for Communism. The Gang of Four preferred a system of communist poverty. You accepted our communism then.[1]

In a similar vein, Russia today is incomparably more open as a society than in Soviet times, but it has not crossed a threshold whereby America is no longer concerned with its human-rights abuses. This reality, and the tendency of a universalistic superpower to discount the inevitable divergences of national interests, frustrates the struggle for convergence on such matters as Iran's nuclear programme, or American missile defence.

It is not a bad thing, on balance, that some moral compromises are more difficult for America in the twenty-first century. But it does constrain America's options. Moral imperative more than strategic reckoning pulled the United States into the relatively short war against Libya's Gadhafi regime. A step change in regime violence against civilians might exert a similar pull of American military power into Syria. The age of intervention does not appear, in this context, to be over. To be sure, the fact that no foreign troops entered post-war Libya to secure the fragile peace does suggest that, when it comes to long-term projects of counter-insurgency and nation-building, a certain watershed has been reached. The turn-of-the-century efforts in Bosnia and Kosovo, then Afghanistan and Iraq, probably constituted the high-water marks of American or European willingness to commit ground troops. After Iraq and Afghanistan, there is diminished appetite for lengthy ground campaigns, humanitarian or not.

On such matters, however, the Obama doctrine contains tensions, if not contradictions. The strategy of offshore balancing has great appeal for a superpower that feels depleted by recent land wars; yet the Obama version of it leaves America on the precipice of conflicts with such adversaries as Iran, conflicts that under imaginable scenarios might require ground troops. Likewise, the Obama administration's preference for realist recognition of American limits coexists uneasily with the president's robust assertion that there is an international community with a 'responsibility to protect' civilians against crimes against humanity. The circle can be squared only if the United States has willing and capable partners. Yet such partners are not easy to find. It is to their credit that rising powers such as India and, more recently, China, have been active participants in UN peace-keeping missions. Yet these powers and others, such as Brazil, are profoundly suspicious of Western military interventions, whether in the service of confronting humanitarian outrages, or counter-proliferation. There is no evidence that Chinese, Indian or Brazilian attitudes are changing – at least not on a timescale relevant to this analysis. In the world as we can imagine it for the next quarter-century, America's main diplomatic and strategic partners will remain Europeans. Of course, the pivot to Asia requires a host of regional partners. But it is the Europeans who have joined America in exerting fierce economic and diplomatic pressure against Iran's nuclear programme. It is the Europeans whose economic policies, for better or for worse, will have the greatest effect on the prospects for American recovery. And it was the leading European military powers, especially the United Kingdom and France, who were willing to conduct the air campaign against regime forces in Libya, albeit with Germany's abstention and America's indispensable support.

But it is also the Europeans, alas, whose strategic grasp has atrophied through a degree of post-Cold War complacency and, more recently, economic emergency. The complacency is, in certain respects, understandable. It derives not only from the reality that defence spending almost always goes down after war, but also from the fact that a free-rider problem has long been embedded in the very structure of the alliance. American exasperation with this fact goes back at least to the 1950s, when US Secretary of State John Foster Dulles threatened an 'agonizing reappraisal' if the French National Assembly voted down the European Defence Community. The National Assembly did vote it down, and yet somehow that agonising American reappraisal never came. This was a revealing episode. However much American leaders exhort the Europeans to greater defence efforts, and are disappointed by the response, the United States is unlikely to abandon its allies.

One might argue that the situation is different today: the Cold War is over and American interests are not so directly threatened in Europe. But that actually may be the wrong way to look at things. So long as the United States has a huge military establishment, it is unlikely to be indifferent to what happens in and to Europe. Instinctively, Europeans know this. It is therefore unsurprising, rational and – from their individual national perspectives – even proper that their own defence efforts will be underwhelming. American military hyper-power is the overwhelming reality and the limiting condition for all of the European calculations, debates and even subconscious assumptions underlying Europe's own defence efforts.

Under these circumstances, perhaps the best that can be expected are self-consciously 'teachable moments' such as the Libya intervention, where America said it would take a back seat and actually did so. All in all, the European states, led by France and the UK, rose to the occasion, while maintaining active military commitments elsewhere. And, pervasive Euroscepticism notwithstanding, they may well have set a precedent and a benchmark for future, similar crises.

Europe's response to the economic emergency has been less laudable. The strategic future of the West is undermined by the fact that Europe is committing, to borrow Paul Krugman's words, suicide by austerity.[2] Reducing aggregate demand in the midst of a deep recession is the very definition of suicide. Cutting defence spending is, by the same logic, counterproductive. It is true that planning for balanced budgets over the long run will be necessary, and constrained defence spending will have to be part of that balance. But confidence in that long-run balance is undermined, not helped, by counter-productive spending cuts today.

And yet, while the current economic crisis is unquestionably dire, that does not make it – for the very long term – dispositive. The question for the United States is how long it will take and how much it will cost to put things back in shape. Even Europe will most likely recover, although the future structure of European integration is hard to anticipate. Meanwhile, China is sure to face problems of its own as its current development model runs out of steam, as its financial system becomes more fragile and as its population ages. Historical trend lines rarely continue without interruption. This is hardly the first crisis for the United States; it is also hardly the last.

The current crisis is a wake-up call. American relative decline is real and it is close to inevitable. Ignoring and resisting this reality can cause the corrosive overstretch that pluralists such as Robert Skidelsky, David Calleo, Paul Kennedy and George Kennan have warned against. The lesson emerging both from the United States and from

Europe is that long-term balance is required both in terms of fiscal accounting and in terms of macroeconomic performance. Such long-term balance requires some restraint of US defence spending. At a minimum, this means a realist avoidance of unnecessary wars. More ambitiously, it means taking seriously what Obama declared on the eve of the Libyan intervention – that true leadership consists of creating the conditions within which other countries can shoulder responsibilities as well. These other countries include diverse powers going well beyond America's treaty allies in Europe.

The plurality of power

Such prescriptions will be hard to put into practice. The most pressing challenge will be to identify which conflicts are best avoided. Iran's persistent efforts to develop nuclear capabilities, which would mean at least latent nuclear-weapons capabilities, might be interpreted as one ineluctable aspect of the emerging pluralised world. Indeed, global multipolarity was manifest early in the post-war period with nuclear tests by China and France. Though some in Israel consider Iran's following suit to pose an existential threat, historical perspective would seem to offer a better guide, as James Dobbins recently argued:

> The United States successfully deterred a much more powerful Soviet Union for over 40 years. Some argue that Iran is different, that its leaders are irrational, and that the threat of devastating retaliation would not dissuade it from employing or threatening to employ nuclear weapons.

While this fear is understandable, given occasionally heated Iranian rhetoric, there is nothing in the Islamic Republic's actual behaviour throughout its existence to substantiate the charge of irrationality, let alone suicidal lunacy. Ayatollah Khamenei and President Mahmoud Ahmadinejad, whatever their other flaws, are models of mental health and restrained behaviour compared to Joseph Stalin or Mao Zedong.[3]

President Obama has declared, however, that containment of an Iran armed with nuclear weapons is not an option.[4] This may have been a necessary measure of alliance management and reassurance *vis-à-vis* Israel, and it may reflect a reasonable reading of vital US national interest. It is certainly the case that the current administration hopes to prevent Iran's emergence as a nuclear-weapons state through diplomacy rather than force. But the president has laid down a commitment that may have to be redeemed – either by himself or a successor – with military force. And while there are plausible scenarios for military options that are surgical and short-lived, there are equally plausible scenarios of broader conflict and prolonged war. These scenarios pose the most immediate obstacle to an American strategy of off-shore balancing.[5]

Then there are categories of states that are neither direct adversaries nor reliable partners; these also pose obstacles to any managed devolution of American responsibilities. Pakistan perhaps most clearly embodies this frustrating ambiguity. As the US draws down its military presence in

Afghanistan, it will necessarily refocus its attention on anti-terrorist operations. The Afghan military and police will assume responsibility for law and order in the country, but the United States will not allow Afghanistan to evolve into a safe haven for al-Qaeda or other like-minded groups. The US military will continue to operate in the tribal lands across the border with Pakistan as well, using drone strikes to inflict targeted killings on the al-Qaeda leadership even at the risk of collateral damage to Pakistani civilians. US military action in Pakistan will remain a source of provocation and yet a substantial US military presence in Afghanistan will not be present to encourage restraint. Should elements in Pakistan strike out at residual deployments of US military advisers or, what is more likely, foster insurgencies into Afghanistan that attack US military interests, the administration – whether headed by Obama or Mitt Romney – will have to measure its response. The problem for the United States as it transmutes policy from Afghan counter-insurgency to risk-mitigation will be to minimise Pakistani disruptive behaviour as part of the broader task of getting all neighbours to adopt more benign roles towards Afghanistan.

One of those neighbours is China, the rise of which poses of course a much longer-term challenge. The US will balance and be balanced against. On the whole it might be reasonable to argue that the long-term suspicions of countries such as India, Japan, Russia, the Republic of Korea and the members of ASEAN will tend to be aimed more in the direction of China than the US. In this regard, multi-polarity in Asia is structured – or at least can be structured – largely in America's favour. Yet these Asian countries have made it clear, repeatedly, that they do not want to be placed in a position of being forced to choose overtly between the two Pacific powers. This is a situation requiring adept diplomacy as well as strategic staying power from the United States, which must respond to what Adam Ward has dubbed 'strategic import demand' from other Asian states while not promoting a zero-sum competition or destabilising arms race with China.[6] US Secretary of Defense Leon Panetta was among the most recent US officials to try to define the narrow space between American 'rebalancing' in Asia-Pacific and a more aggressive 'containment' policy against Beijing.

> Some view the increased emphasis by the United States on the Asia-Pacific region as some kind of challenge to China. I reject that view entirely. Our effort to renew and intensify our involvement in Asia is fully compatible – fully compatible – with the development and growth of China. Indeed, increased U.S. involvement in this region will benefit China as it advances our shared security and prosperity for the future.[7]

Getting the balance right is obviously an overriding demand on US strategy and diplomacy. Along with the danger of provoking Beijing with a posture that might appear aggressive, the obverse risk is that the spectre of American disarray and decline could embolden nationalists in a still-growing China to demand more aggressive and assertive policies. In theory, such assertiveness would be enabled by the possibility that China's GDP and military spending could exceed America's by the middle of the century. Yet, we should not let hypothetical future dangers scare us out of recognising some stabilising realities of the present. 'China', Dobbins observes, 'is seeking neither territorial aggrandisement nor ideological sway over its neighbours. It shows no interest in matching US military expenditures, achieving comparable global reach, or assuming defence commitments beyond its immediate periphery'.[8] Indeed, insofar as Beijing is not eager to be a supplier of global public goods, its grand strategy at least implicitly confers upon the United States a continued leadership role. All of this might change, of course, but the United States would have ample time to observe these changes and adjust its own strategic planning and posture.

There are other emerging powers whose partnership with the United States should be achievable and manageable, but can hardly be taken for granted. The Obama administration has done a good job in recognising and exploiting NATO ally Turkey's more assertive diplomacy in the Middle East, even as the quasi-Gaullist tendencies of Turkish leaders put the country at odds with mainstream US opinion on matters including Israel and Iran. A partnership with India has become deeply anchored in political and cultural affinities even as New Delhi maintains very different visions of international order. Brazil's emergence offers the prospect of a Latin America at once friendly with the United States and less encumbered by a historical legacy of US meddling.

Thus it is hardly inevitable that the United States will find itself besieged or alone. There are significant areas where Washington should be able to find partners and allies to call upon. The European Union seems too disunited as this book goes to press to forge a common policy towards North Africa, and nor is Turkey in a position to handle the Syria crisis on its own. Nevertheless, these powerful regional actors have powerful immediate interests in stabilising their borders, if only to prevent an influx of immigrants or refugees from their own near abroad. These are areas where American leadership can make a difference in shaping the conditions for others to shoulder responsibility – much as the George W. Bush administration allowed the European Union to take point when Russia invaded Georgia in 2008.

Other regional powers can also be encouraged to play a more prominent role in patrolling the Indian Ocean to fend off the predations of Somali pirates and in the perennial battle against international organised crime. These are areas where all states have an interest in having a constabulary role performed. Of course, many of these countries would be happy to see the United States continuing to shoulder a disproportionate share of the burdens in protecting global trade; against such free-riding, future administrations will have to push hard.

The situation becomes more complicated when very large regional actors like India and China become involved – particularly when they become involved with one another. This could be a future administration's greatest challenge because it means finding common cause with each of these fast emerging world powers; it also means accepting the possibility that they may find enough in common to balance against the United States. Environmental negotiations are a good example. India and China reject US calls for less energy-intensive development until richer countries such as the United States offer some economic compensation for the damage they have already caused.

Accommodating these rising powers will be difficult, both when they forge a united front against the United States and when they come into conflict with one another. This challenge of adapting to a more plural world cannot be avoided and it should not be viewed as a 'problem'. The fact that hundreds of millions of people are being elevated out of poverty and brought into the world economy is cause for celebration. Future administrations will have to adapt to the competition for resources and the redistribution of economic activity, but the costs are worth paying when compared to the unstable alternative of an increasingly inequitable world. Hence the challenge is as much domestic as international. It depends upon the ability of the United States to accept and redistribute these adjustment costs. First and foremost, this means that future administrations will have to admit that globalisation creates losers as well as winners within the American economy, and they will have to forge agreement on how those consequences can be managed fairly and without leaving the inevitable losers to fend for themselves.

The primacy of politics

Unfortunately, this domestic adaptation to a more plural world economy may confront future governments in a weakened state. America's most acute problem is a self-inflicted political decline.

The United States could be facing a genuine constitutional crisis. Its eighteenth-century constitution, with a radical separation of powers and multiple veto points, has always required a degree of political consensus across the parties. Episodes where this consensus broke down included the events leading to the American Civil War. That war left its mark: the present-day map of political polarisation closely follows the 1861 line of dissolution. In recent years, it is mainly the Republicans who have used the machinery of checks and balances to create gridlock, but there is little reason to doubt that when the roles are reversed, Democrats will be tempted to follow the same logic.

It is not obvious, in other words, how America will escape its current political paralysis. Leadership on climate change looks unlikely – yet failure to lead could be catastrophic. Economic revival will be difficult – yet that revival is a prerequisite to most other goals, foreign and domestic. Balance, of savings and investment as well as government revenue and government expenditure, will be hard to achieve – yet balance is what is needed for America to sustain a decent domestic society and a responsible world role. If Barack Obama is re-elected, he will continue to face a fiercely rejectionist Republican opposition, and will probably have to settle for incremental progress toward the goals that were boldly proclaimed in 2008. If Romney defeats the incumbent president, he will be driven by an emboldened, very conservative Republican Party to confront resentful Democrats with long memories. He would do well, if political circumstance allows, to rediscover the centrist, progressive persona of his Massachusetts governorship.

Neither scenario would be conducive to any radical departure from the core traditions of American foreign policy. No

US government will renounce the claim to global leadership, and no American president will deny that the United States has an exceptional role in history. But the foreign policies of the next decades, to be successful, will need to accommodate both American idealism and common-sense realism, in a world where the distribution of power is increasingly plural. Polarisation at home does not make this challenge any easier. A bitterly divided America is less attractive for other countries to follow. After a decade of spectacular terrorism, divisive war and economic trauma, the American state and society will struggle to restore the national self-confidence that can sustain an inclusive and equitable position of global leadership. Still, historical reflection and patriotic conviction lead us to a somewhat hopeful conclusion. We would not bet on failure.

APPENDIX

American power in decline?

Table 1 **US national defense budget authority FY2010–FY2012**

(US$million)	2010	2011 Continuing Resolution			2012 Request		
		Base + Enacted	OCO Supplemental Request	Total	Base	Overseas Contingency Operations	Total
Military Personnel	157,100	140,131	16,643	156,774	148,304	11,229	159,532
Operations & Maintenance	293,630	185,307	109,648	294,956	205,259	90,761	296,020
Procurement	135,817	104,789	29,375	134,164	113,028	15,022	128,050
R D T & E	80,234	80,387	518	80,905	75,425	397	75,822
Military Construction	22,577	15,920	1,399	17,319	13,072	0	13,072
Family Housing	2,267	2,272	0	2,272	1,694	0	1,694
Other	4,022	24,817	1,449	26,266	1,109	435	1,544
Total Department of Defense	**695,646**	**553,623**	**159,033**	**712,656**	**557,891**	**117,843**	**675,734**
Department of Energy (defence-related)	18,233			19,039			19,281
Other (defence-related)	7,430			7,622			7,791
Total National Defense	**721,309**			**739,317**			**702,806**

Source: *The Military Balance 2012*

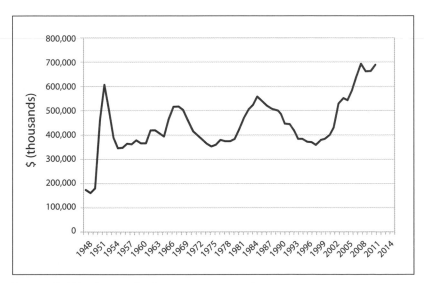

Figure 1 **DoD budget authority** (Constant FY2010 $)

Source: http://comptroller.defense.gov/Budget2010.html, *The Military Balance 2012*

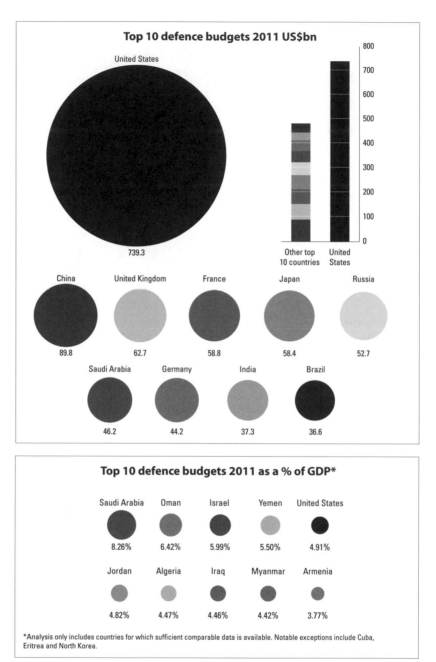

Figure 2: **Comparative defence statistics**

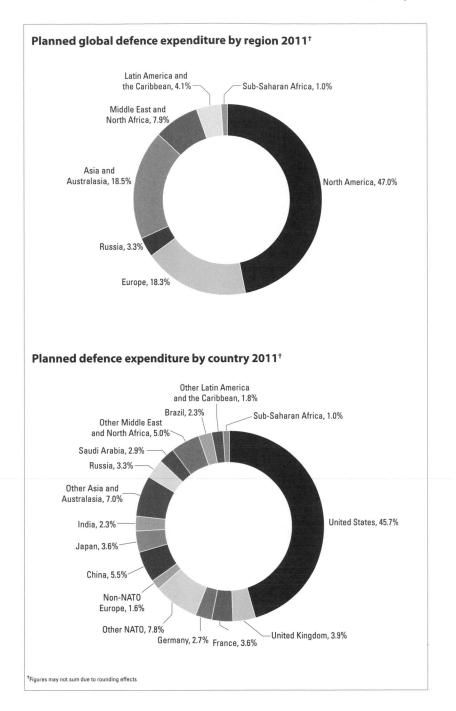

Planned global defence expenditure by region 2011†

Latin America and the Caribbean, 4.1%

Sub-Saharan Africa, 1.0%

Middle East and North Africa, 7.9%

Asia and Australasia, 18.5%

North America, 47.0%

Russia, 3.3%

Europe, 18.3%

Planned defence expenditure by country 2011†

Other Latin America and the Caribbean, 1.8%

Brazil, 2.3%

Other Middle East and North Africa, 5.0%

Sub-Saharan Africa, 1.0%

Saudi Arabia, 2.9%

Russia, 3.3%

Other Asia and Australasia, 7.0%

United States, 45.7%

India, 2.3%

Japan, 3.6%

China, 5.5%

Non-NATO Europe, 1.6%

Other NATO, 7.8%

Germany, 2.7%   France, 3.6%

United Kingdom, 3.9%

†Figures may not sum due to rounding effects

Table 2 **Budget authority for Iraq, Afghanistan, and other overseas contingency operations FY2001–FY2011 (US$bn)**

Operation and Source of Funding	FY01 & FY02	FY03	FY04	FY05	FY06	FY07	FY08	FY09	FY10	FY11 CRA	FY12 Pending Request	Cumulative Total FY01–FY12 incl. CRA/Request
Iraq												
Dept of Defense	0	50.0	56.4	83.4	98.1	127.2	138.5	92.0	66.5	45.7	10.6	768.8
Foreign Aid & Diplomatic Operations	0	3.0	19.5	2.0	3.2	3.2	2.7	2.2	3.3	2.3	6.2	47.6
VA Medical	0	0	0	0.2	0.4	0.9	0.9	1.2	1.5	1.3	0.9	7.2
Total Iraq	0.0	53.0	75.9	85.6	101.7	131.3	142.1	95.5	71.3	49.3	17.7	823.2
Afghanistan												
Dept of Defense	20.0	14.0	12.4	17.2	17.9	37.2	40.6	56.1	87.7	113.3	107.3	523.5
Foreign Aid & Diplomatic Operations	0.8	0.7	2.2	2.8	1.1	1.9	2.7	3.1	5.7	4.1	4.3	29.4
VA Medical	0	0	0	0	0	0.1	0.1	0.2	0.5	1.1	2.1	4.2
Total Afghanistan	20.8	14.7	14.6	20.0	19.0	39.2	43.4	59.5	93.8	118.6	113.7	557.1
Enhanced Security												
Dept of Defense	13.0	8.0	3.7	2.1	0.8	0.5	0.1	0.1	0.1	0.1	0.1	28.7
Total Enhanced Security	13.0	8.0	3.7	2.1	0.8	0.5	0.1	0.1	0.1	0.1	0.1	28.7
DOD Unallocated	0	5.5	0	0	0	0	0	0	0	0	0	5.5
Total All Missions	33.8	81.1	94.1	107.6	121.5	170.9	185.6	155.1	165.3	168.1	131.6	1,414.8

Source: CRS Report RL33110; *The Military Balance 2012*

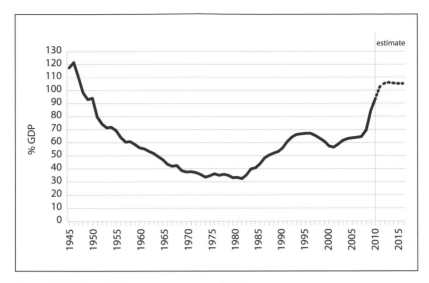

Figure 3 **US federal debt as percentage of GDP**

Source: http://www.gpo.gov/fdsys/pkg/BUDGET-2012-TAB/pdf/BUDGET-2012-TAB.pdf

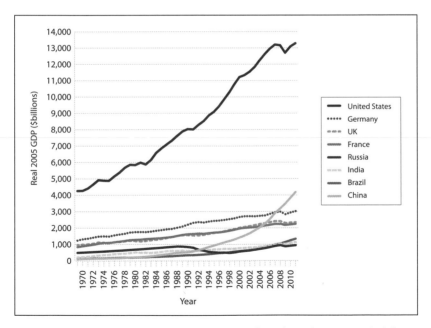

Figure 4 **Real historical gross domestic product for selected countries** (in billions of 2005 dollars)

Source: World Bank World Development Indicators, International Financial Statistics of the IMF, IHS Global Insight, and Oxford Economic Forecasting, as well as estimated and projected values developed by the Economic Research Service all converted to a 2005 base year.

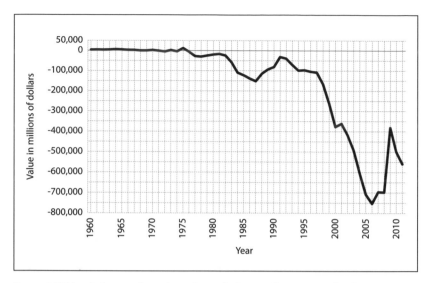

Figure 5 **US trade in goods and services – balance of payments basis**

Note: Data presented on a Balance of Payment (BOP) basis. Information on data sources and methodology are available at www.census.gov/foreign-trade/www/press.html. Source: U.S. Census Bureau, Foreign Trade Division.

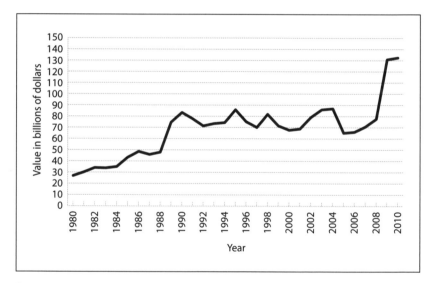

Figure 6 **US reserve assets**

In billions of dollars (100 represents $100,000,000,000). Source: U.S. Department of the Treasury.

NOTES

Introduction

1   'President Obama's Address on the War in Afghanistan', *New York Times*, 1 December 2009, http://www.nytimes.com/2009/12/02/world/asia/02prexy.text.html.

2   J. William Fulbright, *The Arrogance of Power* (New York: Random House, 1966).

3   'An American Century: A Strategy to Secure America's Enduring Interests and Ideals,' A Romney for President White Paper (7 October 2011).

4   Robert Kagan, 'Power and Weakness', *Policy Review*, June and July 2002, pp. 3–28.

5   Robert Kagan, *Dangerous Nation* (New York: Alfred A. Knopf, 2006).

6   The original quote was made on NBC's 'Today Show' on 19 February 1998. Albright was responding to Matt Lauer's question about whether she would be willing to use force against Saddam Hussein. Her answer was as follows: 'It is the threat of the use of force and our line-up there that is going to put force behind the diplomacy. But if we have to use force, it is because we are America; we are the indispensable nation. We stand tall and we see further than other countries into the future, and we see the danger here to all of us.' That transcript is available at: http://www.cryptome.org/jya/see-far.htm.

7   Francis Fukuyama, *America at the Crossroads: Democracy, Power, and the Neoconservative Legacy* (New Haven, CT: Yale University Press, 2007). See also James Mann, *Rise of the Vulcans: The History of Bush's War Cabinet* (New York: Viking, 2004).

8   The iconic illustration of this attitude was General Scowcroft's 4 August 2002 interview on CBS's 'Face the Nation' when he made the case against war in Iraq. The transcript of that interview can be found at: http://www.cbsnews.com/stories/2002/08/05/ftn/main517523.shtml.

9   The latest recent contribution from Nye is Joseph S. Nye, Jr, *The Future of Power* (New York: Public Affairs, 2011); for Huntington, see Samuel P. Hungtington, *The Clash of Civilisations and the Remaking of World Order* (New York: Touchstone, 1997).

10 See Ron Suskind, *The One Percent Doctrine: Deep Inside America's Pursuit of Its Enemies Since 9/11* (New York: Simon & Schuster, 2006).

11 Powell's faith in the so-called 'Pottery Barn rule' was reported in Bob Woodward, *Plan of Attack* (New York: Simon & Schuster, 2004), p. 150.

12 See: http://www.csis.org/program/smart-power-initiative.

13 See: http://www.princeton.edu/~ppns/.

14 Paul Kennedy, *The Rise and Fall of Great Powers: Economic Change and Military Conflict from 1500 to 2000* (New York: Random House, 1987).

15 David P. Calleo and Benjamin M. Rowland, *America and the World Political Economy: Atlantic Dreams and National Realities* (Bloomington, IN: Indiana University Press, 1973); Robert Gilpin, *U.S. Power and the Multinational Corporation: The Political Economy of Foreign Direct Investment* (New York: Basic Books, 1975).

16 This is an allusion to John Gerard Ruggie, 'International Regimes, Transactions, and Change: Embedded Liberalism in the Postwar Economic Order', *International Organisation* vol. 62, no. 2, Spring 1982, pp. 379–415.

17 Stephen S. Cohen and J. Bradford DeLong, *The End of Influence: What Happens When Other Countries Have the Money* (New York: Basic Books, 2010).

18 The reference to 'the wellspring' is taken from the Obama administration's May 2010 *National Security Strategy*. See http://www.whitehouse.gov/sites/default/files/rss_viewer/national_security_strategy.pdf.

19 Fareed Zakaria, *The Post-American World* (New York: W.W. Norton & Company, 2008); Thomas Friedman, *The World is Flat: A Brief History of the Twenty-First Century* (New York: Picador, 2007).

20 Henry Kissinger, *On China* (New York: Penguin, 2011).

21 Ian Bremmer, *Every Nation for Itself: Winners and Losers in a G-zero World* (New York: Portfolio, 2012); Charles A. Kupchan, *No One's World: The West, the Rising Rest, and the Coming Global Turn* (New York: Oxford University Press for the Council on Foreign Relations, 2012).

22 G. John Ikenberry, *Liberal Leviathan: The Origins, Crisis and Transformation of the American World Order* (Princeton, NJ: Princeton University Press, 2011); Robert O. Keohane, *After Hegemony: Cooperation and Discord in the World Political Economy* (Princeton, NJ: Princeton University Press, 1984).

23 *Ibid.*, pp. 334, 335.

24 Barry Eichengreen, *Exorbitant Privilege: The Rise and Fall of the Dollar and the Future of the International Monetary System* (New York: Oxford University Press, 2011).

25 Michael Mandelbaum, *The Frugal Superpower: America's Global Leadership in a Cash-Strapped Era* (New York: Public Affairs, 2010); Michael O'Hanlon, *The Wounded Giant: America's Armed Forces in an Age of Austerity* (New York: Penguin, 2011); Rachel Maddow, *Drift: The Unmooring of American Military Power* (New York: Crown Publishers, 2012).

26 Jack Goldsmith, *Power and Constraint: The Accountable Presidency after 9/11* (New York: W.W. Norton & Co., 2012).

27 Edward Luce, *Time to Start Thinking: America in the Age of Descent* (New York: Atlantic Monthly Press, 2012).

28 Cohen and De Long, *The End of Influence*.

29 Thomas L. Friedman and Michael Mandelbaum, *That Used to Be Us: How America Fell Behind in the World It Invented and How We Can Come Back* (New York: Farrar, Straus and Giroux, 2011).

30 Robert Kagan, *The World America Made* (New York: Alfred A. Knopf, 2012).

31 Joseph S. Nye Jr, *The Future of Power* (New York: Public Affairs, 2011).

32 Richard N. Haass, 'The Restoration Doctrine', *The American Interest* January/February 2012.

33 Robert Kagan, *The World America Made* (New York: Alfred A. Knopf, 2012).

34 'National Security Strategy', (Washington DC: The White House, May 2010), p. 2.

Chapter One

1 Doris Kearns Goodwin, *Team of Rivals: The Political Genius of Abraham Lincoln* (London: Penguin Books, 2009), pp. 120–22.

2 John L. Harper, 'Anatomy of a Habit: America's Unnecessary Wars', *Survival*, vol. 47, no. 2, Summer 2005, pp. 47–86 (2005).

3 Robert Kagan, *Dangerous Nation: American and the World, 1600–1898* (London: Atlantic Books, 2006), pp. 224–5.

4 *Ibid.*, p. 42.

5 Gary Wills, *Lincoln at Gettysburg: The Words That Remade America* (New York: Simon & Schuster, 1992). The Gettysburg Address was part of a dedication ceremony for the Soldiers' National Cemetery in Gettysburg, Pennsylvania. The cemetery was the final resting place for up to 51,000 soldiers from both the Union and the Confederate armies, who had fallen four months

earlier in the Battle of Gettysburg, when Lincoln's generals halted the Confederates' invasion of the north and began to turn the tide of the war.

6 From a speech by John Quincy Adams, to mark Independence Day in 1821, available at http://www.fff.org/comment/AdamsPolicy.asp.

7 Our thinking on the geopolitical importance of a unified United States has been influenced by conversations with a number of colleagues including, notably, Steven Simon.

8 Kagan, *Dangerous Nation,* p. 226.

9 Robert Kagan, 'The World and President Bush', *Survival,* vol. 43, no. 1, Spring 2001, p. 8.

10 John L. Harper, *American Visions of Europe: Franklin D. Roosevelt, George F. Kennan, and Dean G. Acheson* (Cambridge and New York: Cambridge University Press, 1994).

11 *Ibid.*

12 *Ibid.,* p. 35.

13 John L. Gaddis, *Strategies of Containment: A Critical Appraisal of Postwar American National Security* (New York: Oxford University Press, 1982), p. 11.

14 Harper, *American visions of Europe,* p. 60.

15 *Ibid.,* pp. 245, 262, 269.

16 *Ibid.,* pp. 275, 276.

17 Harry S. Truman, speech delivered 12 March 1947 before a Joint Session of Congress, http://www.americanrhetoric.com/speeches/harrystrumantrumandoctrine.html.

18 George F. Kennan, *Memoirs 1925–50* (New York: Pantheon Books, 1972), p. 326.

19 *Ibid.,* p. 322.

20 Fredrik Stanton, *Great Negotiations: Agreements That Changed the Modern World* (Yardley, PA: Westholme Publishing, 2010), pp. 23–44.

21 John L. Harper, *American Machiavelli: Alexander Hamilton and the Origins of U.S. Foreign Policy* (Cambridge and New York: Cambridge University Press, 2004), p. 75–87.

22 Speech by James Madison at the Constitutional Convention, 29 June 1787, from Max Farrand, *Records of the Federal Convention of 1787,* vol. 1 (New Haven, CT: Yale University Press, 1911), p. 465.

23 Whether brave or foolhardy, Taft's devotion to principle made a favourable impression on at least one major figure from the opposing party; see John F. Kennedy, *Profiles in Courage* (New York: Pocket Edition, 1961), p. 185.

24 Kennan, *Memoirs 1925–50,* p. 50.

25 Telegram from The Chargé in the Soviet Union to the Secretary of State, 22 February 1946, quoted in *Foreign Relations of the United States, 1946,* vol. vi (Washington DC: US Government Printing Office, 1969), p. 706.

26 Kennan, *Memoirs 1925–50,* p. 411.

27 Harper, *American Visions of Europe,* p. 337.

28 David P. Calleo, *Beyond American Hegemony: the Future of the Western Alliance* (New York: Perseus, 1989), p. 33.

29 'Gallic logic often tempted him to carry his postulates to extremes unnecessarily wounding to Americans', Henry Kissinger, *White House Years* (Boston, MA and Toronto, ON: Little, Brown & Company, 1979), p. 104.

30 After the Berlin Wall was built in 1961, for example, Berlin's Social-Democratic mayor Willy Brandt wrote to Kennedy, saying: 'Inaction or merely defensive action could provoke a crisis of confidence in the Western powers.' Later, Brandt summarised the episode acidly: 'The Soviet Union had defied the major power in the Western world and effectively humiliated it.' See Dana H. Allin, *Cold War Illusions: America, Europe and Soviet Power, 1969–1989* (New York: St. Martin's, 1997) p. 20.

31 Dana H. Allin, 'De Gaulle and American Power', in Benjamin M. Rowland (ed.), *Charles de Gaulle's Legacy of Ideas* (Lanham, MD: Lexington Books, 2011), p. 100.

32 Remarks by Dr Condoleezza Rice, Assistant to the President for National Security Affairs, at the International Institute for Strategic Studies, London, 26 June 2003, available at http://www.iiss.org/recent-key-addresses/condoleezza-rice-address/.

33 William Pfaff, 'The American Mission?', *New York Review of Books*, vol. 51, no.6, 8 April 2004; David P. Calleo, 'The Broken West', *Survival*, vol. 46, no.3, Autmn 2004, p. 33.

34 De Gaulle, cited in David P. Calleo, *Europe's Future: The Grand Alternatives* (New York: Horizon Press, 1965), p. 117

35 Charles de Gaulle, *The Complete War Memoirs of Charles de Gaulle, 1940–46, Vol. 2: Unity* (New York: Simon & Schuster 1964), pp. 573–4.

36 John L. Harper, 'The Road to Phnom Penh – De Gaulle, The Americans and Vietnam 1944–1966', in Rowland (ed.), *Charles de Gaulle's Legacy of Ideas*, p. 54.

37 Richard M. Nixon, 'U.S. Foreign Policy for the 1970s: A New Strategy for Peace', Report to Congress, 18 February 1970 , p. 7.

38 Dana H. Allin and Steven Simon, *The Sixth Crisis: Iran, Israel, America and the Rumours of War* (Oxford and New York: Oxford University Press, 2010), p. 30.

39 William Greider, *Secrets of the Temple: How the Federal Reserve Runs the Country* (New York: Touchstone, 1989), pp. 396, 397 and 400.

40 Greider, *Secrets of the Temple*, pp. 354, 541–2, 574–5.

41 Dana H. Allin, *Cold War Illusions* (New York: St Martin's Press, 1995), p. 174.

42 James M. Goldgeir, *Not Whether But When: The U.S. Decision to enlarge NATO* (Washington D.C.: Brookings Institution Press, 1999), p. 142.

43 Martin Indyk, Graham Fuller, Anthony Cordesman and Phebe Marr, 'Symposium on Dual Containment: US Policy Towards Iran and Iraq', *Middle East Policy*, vol.3, no.1, March 1994, pp. 1–26.

[44] 'Americans are asking, why do they hate us? They hate what we see right here in this chamber – a democratically elected government. Their leaders are self-appointed. They hate our freedoms – our freedom of religion, our freedom of speech, our freedom to vote and assemble and disagree with each other.' George W. Bush, Address to a Joint Session of Congress and the American People, 20 September 2001, http://georgewbush-whitehouse.archives.gov/news/releases/2001/09/20010920-8.html.

[45] Francis Fukuyama, 'Invasion of the Isolationists', New York Times, 31 August 2005.

[46] An American presidential election comprises 50 separate state elections (plus the District of Columbia). Each state has a number of electoral college votes allocated roughly in proportion to its population, and the candidate with the plurality of votes in that state (with two exceptions) wins all its electoral votes. In theory, this means that the loser of the nationwide popular vote can win a majority of electoral votes, and hence the election, as occurred in 2000.

[47] For a brilliant cultural history, see Rick Perlstein, Nixonland: The Rise of a President and the Fracturing of America (New York: Scribner, 2008).

[48] George McGovern, Address Accepting the Presidential Nomination at the Democratic National Convention in Miami Beach, Florida, 14 July 1972, http://www.presidency.ucsb.edu/ws/index.php?pid=25967#axzz1to22VRxA.

[49] Total US defence spending (in inflation-adjusted dollars) has reached levels not seen since the Second World War, when the United States had 12 million people under arms and waged wars on three continents. Moreover, the US share of global military expenditure has jumped from about a third to about half since 2000. Some of this growth can be attributed to the wars in Iraq and Afghanistan, but the baseline or regular defence budget has also increased significantly. It has grown in real terms for an unprecedented 13 straight years, and it is now $100 billion above what the nation spent on average during the Cold War. The fiscal year 2012 budget request of $553bn is approximately the same level as Ronald Reagan's FY 1986 budget. See http://www.americanprogress.org/issues/2011/07/historical_defense_budget.html.

[50] Dwight D. Eisenhower, farewell address, 17 January 1961, at http://avalon.law.yale.edu/20th_century/eisenhower001.asp.

[51] J.L. Gaddis, Strategies of Containment (New York: Oxford University Press, 1982), p. 164; Lawrence J. Korb, Laura Conley and Alex Rothman, 'A Historical Perspective on Defense Budgets', Center for American Progress, 6 July 2011,

http://www.americanprogress.org/issues/2011/07/historical_defense_budget.html.

52 John F. Kennedy, *The Strategy of Peace* (New York: Harper & Row, 1960), pp. 37–8.

53 David P. Calleo, *Beyond American Hegemony: The Future of the Western Alliance* (New York: Basic Books, 1987), pp. 72–3.

54 David Halberstam, *The Best and the Brightest* (New York: Ballantyne Books, [25th anniversary edition], 1992).

55 Gordon M. Goldstein, Lessons in Disaster: McGeorge Bundy and the Path to War in Vietnam (New York: Henry Holt & company, 2008), pp. 229–49.

56 The 'security dilemma' arises when one country takes actions in response to perceived threats to its security that are in turn perceived by a second country as threats to its own security. The second country may then take actions that further threaten the security of the first – whose initial actions thus have the opposite of their intended effect. Yet neither side can afford not to respond to security threats. This can result in arms races or other forms of spiralling insecurity, and in the extreme case, in the outbreak of war.

57 Richard Reeves, *President Kennedy: Profile of Power* (New York: Simon & Schuster, 1993), pp. 305–6.

58 President John F. Kennedy, *Commencement Address at American University*, Washington DC, 10 June 1963, http://www.jfklibrary.org/Research/Ready-Reference/JFK-Speeches/Commencement-Address-at-American-University-June-10-1963.aspx.

59 Allin, *Cold War Illusions*, pp. 53–8.

60 Kennan, *Memoirs*, vol. 1, p. 367.

61 Gaddis, *Strategies of Containment*, p. 283.

62 Henry Kissinger, *White House Years* (London: Little, Brown & Company, 1988), pp. 104–11; Kissinger, 'Central Issues of American Foreign Policy', in Kermit Gordon (ed.), *Agenda for the Nation* (Washington DC: The Brookings Institution, 1968), p. 40.

63 Henry Kissinger, *Years of Upheaval* (Boston, MA: Little, Brown and Company, 1982), pp. 897–8.

64 *Ibid.*, p. 460.

65 The extent of that alignment was impressive, and disquieting: 'US companies sold Iraq precursors useable for chemical weapons, while Washington helped Baghdad locate third-country sources for the purchase of weapons, such as cluster bombs, that the United States was unable to provide; provided satellite intelligence on the positioning of Iran's forces; and reflagged and protected Kuwaiti oil tankers after the Islamic Revolutionary Guard Corps started to attack the Gulf Arab shipping that was helping to finance Iraq's war effort. Moreover, in an ugly irony, given Washington's later

indignation about Saddam's "weapons of mass destruction", the Reagan administration in effect condoned Iraq's strategically significant use of chemical weapons against Iraq.' Allin and Simon, *The Sixth Crisis*, pp. 25–7.

66 George P. Shultz, 'Terrorism and the Modern World', US State Department Bulletin, December 1984, http://findarticles.com/p/articles/mi_m1079/is_v84/ai_3536847/pg_3/; Charles Krauthammer, 'Only in Their Dreams', *Time*, December 2001, http://www.time.com/time/magazine/article/0,9171,1101011224-188565,00.html.

67 John Harper review of Marvin Kalb and Deborah Kalb, *Haunting Legacy: Vietnam and the American Presidency from Ford to Obama*, in *Survival*, vol. 53, no. 6, December 2011–January 2012, p. 209.

68 Colin Powell, 'Why Generals Get Nervous', *New York Times*, 8 October 1992, Late Edition – Final , p. A 35.

69 Dana H. Allin, *NATO's Balkan Interventions*, Adelphi Paper 347 (Oxford: Oxford University Press for the IISS, 2002), pp. 36–40.

Chapter Two

1 See, for example, 'Al Qaeda is Bleeding US to Bankruptcy, Bin Laden Claims', *Guardian*, 3 November 2004, http://www.guardian.co.uk/world/2004/nov/03/usa.alqaida.

2 See Joseph P. Stiglitz, 'The True Cost of 9/11', *Slate Magazine*, 1 September 2011, http://www.slate.com/articles/business/project_syndicate/2011/09/the_true_cost_of_911.single.html.

3 Ezra Klein, 'Osama Bin Laden Didn't Win, but he Was "Enormously Successful"', *Washington Post*, 3 May 2011, http://www.washingtonpost.com/business/economy/osama-bin-laden-didnt-win-but-he-was-enormously-successful/2011/05/02/AFexZjbF_story.html.

4 See http://www.dlc.org/documents/RebuildingReserves111407.pdf.

5 Klein, 'Osama Bin Laden Didn't Win, but He Was "Enormously Successful"'.

6 Gallup polls on Iraq can be found at: http://www.gallup.com/poll/1633/Iraq.aspx. A survey in late 2011 asked the following question: 'Turning to Iraq, do you approve or disapprove of President Obama's decision to withdraw nearly all U.S. troops from Iraq by the end of the year?' Three quarters said they approved; 21% disapproved; 5% expressed no opinion.

7 Barack Obama, speech given in Chicago, IL, 2 October 2002, transcript available at http://www. economics.utoronto.ca/munro5/ObamaonIraqOct2002.pdf.

8 See, for example, Philip H. Gordon, *Winning the Right War: The Path to Security for America and the World*, (New York: Times Books, Henry Holt and Company, 2007), pp. 4, 26–27, 107.

9 From the first presidential debate between George W. Bush and John Kerry, 30 September 2004, University of Miami, Florida. A transcript is available at http://www.debates.org/index.php?page=september-30-2004-debate-transcript.

10 From the first presidential debate between John McCain and Barack Obama, 26 September 2008, Unibversity of Mississippi, Oxford, Mississippi. Available at http://www.debates.org/index.php?page=2008-debate-transcript.

11 Michael R. Gordon, 'The 2000 Campaign: The Military; Bush Would Stop U.S. Peacekeeping In Balkan Fights', *New York Times*, 21 October 2000, http://www.nytimes.com/2000/10/21/us/the-2000-campaign-the-military-bush-would-stop-us-peacekeeping-in-balkan-fights.html.

12 From the second presidential debate between George W. Bush and Al Gore, 11 October 2000, Wake Forest University, North Carolina, http://www.debates.org/index.php?page=october-11-2000-debate-transcript.

13 The 9th IISS Asia Security Summit, The Shangri-La Dialogue, Singapore, Saturday 5 June 2010, First Plenary Session, Strengthening Security Partnerships in the Asia-Pacific, Robert M. Gates, Secretary of Defense, United States, http://www.iiss.org/conferences/the-shangri-la-dialogue/shangri-la-dialogue-2010/plenary-session-speeches/first-plenary-session/robert-gates/.

14 H.R. McMaster, 'On War: Lessons to be Learned', *Survival*, vol. 50, no. 1, February–March 2008, pp. 19–30.

15 James Dobbins, Seth G. Jones, Keith Crane and Beth Cole DeGrasse, *A Beginner's Guide to Nation-Building* (Santa Monica, CA: Rand Corporation, 2007), http://www.rand.org/content/dam/rand/pubs/monographs/2007/RAND_MG557.pdf.

16 McMaster, 'On War: Lessons to be Learned'.

17 Steven E. Miller, personal communication with the authors. See also Steven E. Miller, 'The Flawed Case for Missile Defence', Survival, vol. 43, no. 3 (Autumn 2001), pp. 105–6, in which Miller discusses regimicide as a deterrent policy. 'The United States will need to deter any WMD threat that materialises in the future, whether missile-related or not. It should be made clear that the United States will respond ferociously to any

use of WMD against its territory, its forces, or its allies. Against the so-called rogue threat, the United States should declare a deterrent policy of "regimicide": any regime that uses WMD against the United States will not survive. Because of its enormous military superiority, the United States can credibly make such a threat. Because any large-scale WMD use would be so heinous and so galvanising, the likelihood that this threat would be implemented in response is quite high.'

[18] See Alexander Nicoll, 'The Road to Lisbon', in Toby dodge and Nicholas Redman (eds), *Afghanistan: To 2015 and Beyond* (London: Routledge for the IISS, 2011), pp. 26–44.

[19] Bob Woodward, *Obama's Wars* (New York: Simon & Schuster, 2010).

[20] Bob Woodward, 'McChrystal: More Forces or Mission Failure', *Washington Post*, 21 September 2009, http://www.washingtonpost.com/wp-dyn/content/article/2009/09/20/AR2009092002920.html.

[21] General Stanley McChrystal, address at IISS London, 1 October 2009, http://www.iiss.org/recent-key-addresses/general-stanley-mcchrystal-address/.

[22] Woodward, *Obama's Wars*, p. 194.

[23] Obama's 'terms sheet' was published in Woodward, *Obama's Wars;* for these quotations see p. 388.

[24] See, for example, Eliot A. Cohen, 'A Wartime President', *Wall Street Journal*, 9 December 2009, http://online.wsj.com/article/SB100014240527487041071045745714442498 09148.html; Senator John McCain, Interview for ABC News, 'This Week', 7 April 2010, video available online at http://abcnews.go.com/ThisWeek/video/senator-john-mccain-war-afghanistan-general-petraeus-11084520; transcript available online at http://abcnews.go.com/ThisWeek/week-transcript-mccain/story?id=11083929; Senator Lindsey Graham interview with CBS News, 'Face The Nation', 4 July 2010, transcript available at http://www.cbsnews.com/htdocs/pdf/FTN_070410.pdf.

[25] See, for example, Andrew J. Bacevich, 'Non-Believer', *The New Republic*, 7 July 2010, http://www.tnr.com/blog/foreign-policy/76091/non-believer.

[26] Woodward, *Obama's Wars*, p. 390.

[27] *Ibid.*, p. 325.

[28] Defense Secretary Leon Panetta expanded on this theme during a speech to the IISS Shangri-La Dialogue on 2 June 2012. A transcript of his speech, 'The US Rebalance Towards the Asia-Pacific', is available at http://www.iiss.org/conferences/the-shangri-la-dialogue/shangri-la-dialogue-2012/speeches/first-plenary-session/leon-panetta/.

[29] The US justified its invasion of Afghanistan under Article 51 of the UN charter, the right to self-defence. According to the UN Human Rights Council Report

of the Special Rapporteur on extrajudicial, summary or arbitrary executions, the right to self-defence extends to the extra-territorial use of drones, as long as the target is deemed 'lawful' by drone pilots, and the 'requirements of necessity, proportionality and discrimination are met'. See 'Report of the Special Rapporteur on extrajudicial, summary or arbitrary executions, Philip Alston, Study on targeted killing', UN Human Rights Council Report to the UN General Assembly, A/HRC/14/24/Add.6, 28 May 2010, paragraph 93, http://www2.ohchr.org/english/bodies/hrcouncil/docs/14session/A.HRC.14.24.Add6.pdf.

30 Evidence of America's loss of reputation abroad can be seen in a poll published by the Pew Research Center's Global Attitudes Project, 29 July 2010, http://pewglobal.org/2010/07/29/concern-about-extremist-threat-slips-in-pakistan/.

31 On 24 April 1980, the mission ordered by President Carter to rescue hostages from the US embassy in Tehran ended with a fiery disaster in the desert. After a sand storm led to the decision to abort the mission, one of the departing helicopters crashed into a fuel-laden C-130 Hercules transport aircraft; a fire erupted and eight servicemen lost their lives.

32 Peter Beinart, 'Obama's Foreign Policy Doctrine Finally Emerges with "Offshore Balancing"', *The Daily Beast*, 28 November 2011, http://www.thedailybeast.com/articles/2011/11/28/obama-s-foreign-policy-doctrine-finally-emerges-with-off-shore-balancing.html.

33 David P. Calleo, review of Daniel W. Drezner (ed.), *Avoiding Trivia: the Role of Strategic Planning in American Foreign Policy* in *Survival*, vol. 52, no.5 , October–November 2010, p. 233.

34 See Robert E. Hunter, 'A New American Middle East Strategy', *Survival*, vol. 50, no. 6, December 2008–January 2009, p. 61.

35 'The actions that I will take will be actions recommended and supported by Israeli leaders'; Mitt Romney in interview for Israel Hayom, Newsletter, October 28, 2011, available online at http://www.israelhayom.com/site/newsletter_article.php?id=1601.

36 Newt Gingrich interview with The Jewish Channel, 9 December 2011, http://www.youtube.com/watch?v=dHWJWJocD6A; '"Palestinians Are an Invented People", Says Newt Gingrich', *Guardian*, 9 December 2011, http://www.guardian.co.uk/world/2011/dec/10/palestinians-invented-people-newt-gingrich.

37 'Remarks by the President on a New Beginning', Cairo University, Cairo, Egypt, 4 June 2009, http://www.whitehouse.gov/the-press-office/remarks-president-cairo-university-6-04-09.

38 'Speaker Boehner to Invite Israeli Prime Minister Netanyahu to Address Congress', Press Release, Speaker Boehner Press Office, 13 April 2011, http://www.speaker.gov/press-release/speaker-boehner-invite-israeli-prime-minister-netanyahu-address-congress; 'Remarks by the President on the Middle East and North Africa', State Department, Washington DC, 19 May 2011, http://www.whitehouse.gov/the-press-office/2011/05/19/remarks-president-middle-east-and-north-africa; Ethan Bronner, 'Netanyahu Responds Icily to Obama Remarks', *New York Times*, 19 May 2011, http://www.nytimes.com/2011/05/20/world/middleeast/20mideast.html; 'Remarks by President Obama and Prime Minister Netanyahu of Israel After Bilateral Meeting', Oval Office, 20 May 2011; 'PM Netanyahu Addresses the AIPAC Policy Conference 2011', 23 May 2011, Transcript by Israel Ministry of Foreign Affairs, http://www.mfa.gov.il/MFA/Government/Speeches+by+Israeli+leaders/2011/PM_Netanyahu_addresses_AIPAC_Policy_Conference_23-May-2011.htm; Netanyahu's Speech at AIPAC Conference, May 2011, http://www.cfr.org/israel/netanyahus-speech-aipac-conference-may-2011/p25063; Congressional Record, 112th Congress, 1st Session, vol. 157, no. 72, 24 May 2011, H3348–3351 (Joint Meeting to Hear an Address by His Excellency Binyamin Netanyahu, Prime Minister of Israel), http://www.gpo.gov/fdsys/pkg/CREC-2011-05-24/pdf/CREC-2011-05-24-pt1-PgH3348-2.pdf.

39 David A. Fahrenthold, 'Michele Bachmann, Rick Perry speak to CPAC, as Conservatives Call for Unity', *Washington Post*, 9 Feb 2012; http://www.washingtonpost.com/politics/michele-bachmann-rick-perry-speak-to-cpac-as-conservatives-call-for-unity/2012/02/09/gIQAWmfv1Q_story.html.

40 Author communication with anonymous Pentagon official, London, June 2011.

41 Press announcement for United Nations Security Council Resolution 1973, including a full text of the resolution, 17 March 2011, http://www.un.org/News/Press/docs//2011/sc10200.doc.htm.

42 See Bruce D. Jones, 'Libya and the Responsibilities of Power', *Survival*, vol. 53, no. 3, June–July 2011, p. 52.

43 See 'Remarks by the President in Address to the Nation on Libya', National Defense University, Washington DC, 28 March 2011, http://www.whitehouse.gov/the-press-office/2011/03/28/remarks-president-address-nation-libya.

44 Nobel Lecture by Barack H. Obama, Oslo, 10 December 2009, http://nobelprize.org/nobel_prizes/peace/laureates/2009/obama-lecture_en.html.

45 The original UN Security Council Resolution outlining the

responsibility to protect civilians is number 1674 and was adopted in April 2006. See http://www.un.org/News/Press/docs/2006/sc8710.doc.htm. The General Assembly vote on 14 September 2009 reiterated support for the 'right to protect' norm and for its implementation. See http://globalr2p.org/media/pdf/UNResolutionA63L.80Rev.1.pdf.

46 Ryan Lizza, 'The Consequentialist – How the Arab Spring Remade Obama's Foreign Policy', *New Yorker*, 2 May 2011, http://www.newyorker.com/reporting/2011/05/02/110502fa_fact_lizza?currentPage=allù.

47 Thom Shanker and Eric Schmitt, 'Seeing Limits to "New" Kind of War in Libya', *New York Times*, 21 October 2011, http://www.nytimes.com/2011/10/22/world/africa/nato-war-in-libya-shows-united-states-was-vital-to-toppling-qaddafi.html.

48 *Ibid.*

49 Marc Lynch, 'Helping Syria Without War', *Foreign Policy*, Abu Aardvark's Middle East Blog, 21 February 2012, http://lynch.foreignpolicy.com/posts/2012/02/20/helping_syria_without_war.

50 Walter Russell Mead, *Special Providence: American Foreign Policy and How It Changed the World* (London: Routledge, 2002).

51 John Miller, Interview with Bin Laden, ABC 20/20, ABC News, May 1998, transcript available at http://www.pbs.org/wgbh/pages/frontline/shows/binladen/who/interview.html.

52 Ben Rhode, quoted in *Foreign Policy*, 16 December 2011, http://thecable.foreignpolicy.com/posts/2011/12/16/white_house_we_are_returning_to_a_pre_1990_military_stance_in_the_gulf.

53 James Risen and Mark Mazzetti, 'U.S. Agencies See No Move by Iran to Build a Bomb', *New York Times*, 24 February 2012, http://www.nytimes.com/2012/02/25/world/middleeast/us-agencies-see-no-move-by-iran-tobuild-a-bomb.html.

54 Mark Fitzpatrick, personal communication with author, 2 March 2012.

Chapter Three

1 For Santelli's rant, see http://freedomeden.blogspot.it/2009/02/rick-santelli-tea-party.html.

2 Kate Zernike, *Boiling Mad: Inside Tea Party America* (New York: Times Books, 2010).

3 Gregory Kroger, *Filibustering: A Political History of Obstruction in the House and Senate* (Chicago, IL: University of Chicago Press, 2010).

4 Sean M. Theriault, *Party Polarisation in Congress* (Cambridge: Cambridge University Press, 2008); Thomas E. Mann and Norman J. Ornstein, *It's Even Worse than It Looks: How the American Constitutional System Collided with the New Politics of Extremism* (New York: Basic Books, 2012); Nolan McCarty, Howard Rosenthal and Keith T. Poole, *Polarized America: The Dance of Ideology and Unequal Riches* (Cambridge, MA: MIT Press, 2006).

5 Edward Luce, 'The Neocons Are Back Vying for a Seat in the White House,' *Financial Times*, 29 April 2012.

6 Edward Luce, *Time to Start Thinking: America in the Age of Descent* (New York: Atlantic Monthly Press, 2012).

7 For illustrations of this line of argument, see Bobby Jindal, *Leadership and Crisis* (Washington DC: Regnery Publishing, Inc., 2010), chapter 10; Rick Perry, *Fed Up! Our Fight to Save America from Washington* (New York: Little, Brown and Company, 2010), chapter 5.

8 For an extreme version of this argument, see Charles Murray, 'The Happiness of the People', The 2009 Irving Kristol Lecture, American Enterprise Institute, http://www.aei.org/article/society-and-culture/race-and-gender/the-happiness-of-the-people-speech/.

9 See 'News Conference by President Obama', Palaiz de le Musique et le Congres, Strasbourg, 4 April 2009, http://www.whitehouse.gov/the-press-office/news-conference-president-obama-4042009.

10 Kendra Marr, 'Newt Gingrich Talks Faith – not Affairs – at Cornerstone Church in Texas', Politico, 27 March 2011, http://www.politico.com/news/stories/0311/52023.html.

11 Matthew Yglesias, 'Gingrich Warns America May Become a Secular Atheist Country Dominated by Radical Islamists', Thinkprogress.org, 29 March 2011, http://thinkprogress.org/yglesias/2011/03/29/200379/gingrich-warns-america-may-become-a-secular-atheist-country-dominated-by-radical-islamists/?mobile=nc.

12 Dinesh D'Souza, *The Roots of Obama's Rage* (Washington DC: Regnery Publishing, Inc., 2010).

13 Robert Costa, 'Gingrich: "Obama's Kenyan, Anti-Colonial World View"', National Review Online, 11 September 2010, http://www.nationalreview.com/

corner/246302/gingrich-obama-s-kenyan-anti-colonial-worldview-robert-costa#.

14 Jonathan Capehart, 'How Newt Gingrich Thinks', *Washington Post*, 13 September 2010, http://voices.washingtonpost.com/postpartisan/2010/09/how_gingrich_thinks.html.

15 Glenn Kessler, 'Huckabee's "Kenyan Clarification" Raises More Questions', *Washington Post*, 2 March 2011, http://voices.washingtonpost.com/fact-checker/2011/03/huckabees_kenya_clarification.html.

16 'Huckabee Defends Rev. Jeremiah Wright', *Huffington Post*, 28 March 2008, http://www.huffingtonpost.com/2008/03/19/huckabee-defends-rev-jere_n_92346.html.

17 Desmond S. King and Rogers M. Smith, *Still a House Divided: Race and Politics in Obama's America* (Princeton, NJ: Princeton University Press, 2011).

18 McCarty, Rosenthal and Poole, *Polarized America*; King and Smith, *Still a House Divided*.

19 For top marginal tax rate data, see http://www.taxpolicycenter.org/taxfacts/displayafact.cfm?Docid=213.

20 David A. Stockman, *The Triumph of Politics: The Inside Story of the Reagan Revolution* (New York: Avon Books, 1987).

21 Thomas Frank, *The Wrecking Crew: How Conservatives Ruined Government, Enriched Themselves, and Beggared the Nation* (New York: Henry Holt and Company, 2008).

22 The Taxpayer Protection Pledge is available at http://www.atr.org/userfiles/Congressional_pledge(1).pdf.

23 Mann and Ornstein, *It's Even Worse than it Looks*.

24 Though they might also require a filibuster-proof supermajority in the Senate to make good on this promise.

25 David Corn, *Showdown: The Inside Story of How Obama Fought Back Against Boehner, Cantor, and the Tea Party* (New York: William Morrow, 2012).

26 Benyamin Appelbaum and Eric Dash, 'US Debt Downgraded by SP', *New York Times*, 5 August 2011, http://www.nytimes.com/2011/08/06/business/us-debt-downgraded-by-sp.html.

27 See 'Kaiser Commission on Medicaid and the Uninsured' (Washington DC: the Henry J. Kaiser Family Foundation, 2005).

Chapter Four

1 Robert Kagan, 'Not Fade Away: The Myth of American Decline', *The New Republic,* 11 January 2012, http://www.tnr.com/article/politics/magazine/99521/america-world-power-declinism.

2 See Paul Krugman, 'A Dark Age of Macroeconomics', *New York Times,* 27 January 2009, http://krugman.blogs.nytimes.com/2009/01/27/a-dark-age-of-macroeconomics-wonkish/.

3 'In the long run,' Keynes continued, 'we are all dead. Economists set themselves too easy, too useless a task, if in tempestuous seasons they can only tell us that when the storm is long past the sea is flat again.' Keynes, 'A Tract on Monetary Reform' (1923), cited in Robert Skidelsky, *Keynes: The Return of the Master* (London: Allen Lane, 2009), back cover.

4 The National Bureau for Economic Research (NBER) provides the economic profession's official count of business cycles. They list 11 such cycles since 1945. See http://www.nber.org/cycles.html. Only the first ten of these were conventional boom-and-bust cycles. The eleventh was worse.

5 The basic psychology described here is best analysed by Hyman Minsky who derived his 'financial stability hypothesis' reading of Keynes. Charles Kindleberger has popularised this argument through his classic work on financial crises – which has recently been updated to include the most recent crisis by Robert Aliber. See Hyman P. Minsky, *Stabilizing an Unstable Economy* (New Haven, CT: Yale University Press, 1986); Charles P. Kindleberger and Robert Z. Aliber, *Manias, Panics, and Crashes: A History of Financial Crises, Sixth Edition* (London: Palgrave Macmillan, 2011). See also George A. Akerlof and Robert J. Schiller, *Animal Spirits: How Human Psychology Drives the Economy and Why It Matters for Global Capitalism* (Princeton, NJ: Princeton University Press, 2009).

6 See Martin Wolf, *Fixing Global Finance: How to Curb Financial Crises in the 21st Century* (New Haven, CT: Yale University Press, 2009); and Robert J. Schiller, *The Subprime Solution: How Today's Financial Crisis Happened and What to Do about It* (Princeton, NJ: Princeton University Press, 2008).

7 Perhaps the best illustration of this is provided by Michael Lewis, *The Big Short: Inside the Doomsday Machine* (New York: W.W. Norton & Company, 2011).

8 These percentages are calculated using data from the annual macroeconomic database of the European Commission, at http://ec.europa.eu/economy_finance/ameco/user/serie/SelectSerie.cfm.

9 See 'Trends in the Distribution of Household Income between 1979 and 2007' (Washington DC: Congressional Budget Office, 2011).

10 Lewis, *The Big Short*.

11 See Schiller, *The Subprime Solution*. See also Arnold Kling, *Unchecked and Unbalanced* (Lanham, MD: Rowman & Littlefield, 2009).

12 See Hank Paulson, *On the Brink: Inside the Race to Stop the Collapse of the Global Financial System* (New York: Hachette, 2010), pp. 208–22.

13 Two recent industry histories – for Lehman Brothers and AIG – give a sense of the scale of the crisis. See Mark T. Williams, *Uncontrolled Risk* (New York: McGraw-Hill, 2010); Roddy Boyd, *Fatal Risk* (New York: John Wiley & Sons, 2011).

14 The Bureau of Labor Statistics produces a range of indicators to capture the dimensions of what is known technically as 'labour underutilisation', to avoid confusion with the more precise economic definition given to the term unemployment. The figure we quote is for October 2011 and is seasonally adjusted. See http://www.bls.gov/news.release/empsit.t15.htm.

15 See Erik Jones, 'Reconsidering the Role of Ideas in Times of Crisis', in Leila Simona Talani (ed.), *The Global Crash: Towards a New Global Financial Regime?* (London: Palgrave Macmillan, 2010), pp. 52–72.

16 The details for the Geithner plan can be found on the Obama administration's financial stability website at http://www.treasury.gov/press-center/press-releases/Pages/tg65.aspx.

17 See David J. Lynch, 'Economists Agree: Stimulus Created Nearly 3 Million Jobs', *USA Today*, 30 August 2010, http://www.usatoday.com/money/economy/2010-08-30-stimulus30_CV_N.htm; 'Varney Contradicts Private Analysts, Economists with Claim that Stimulus Failed', Media Matters, 7 June 2010, http://mediamatters.org/research/201006070015.

18 See Ezra Klein, 'Could this Time Have Been Different?', *Washington Post*, 25 August 2011, http://www.washingtonpost.com/blogs/ezra-klein/post/could-this-time-have-been-different/2011/08/25/gIQAiJooVL_blog.html; and Paul Krugman, 'Stimulus Arithmetic (Wonkish but Important)', *New York Times*, 6 January 2009, http://krugman.blogs.nytimes.com/2009/01/06/stimulus-arithmetic-wonkish-but-important/.

19 See Jean-Marc Lucas, 'US State and Local Government Finances: From Recession to Austerity' (Paris: BNP Paribas, April 2011), http://economic-research.bnpparibas.com/applis/www/recheco.nsf/ConjonctureByDateEN/50295B95134B87D7C125786F00439852/$File/C1104_A1.pdf.

20 Republican presidential candidates addressed the issue of tax during a debate at Iowa State University,

Arnes, Iowa, 12 August 2011, http://foxnewsinsider.com/2011/08/12/full-transcript-complete-text-of-the-iowa-republican-debate-on-fox-news-channel/. During the debate, Byron York of the *Washington Examiner* asked the candidates: 'Is there any ratio of cuts to taxes that you would accept? Three to one? Four to one? Or even ten to one?' Rick Santorum answered, 'No. The answer is no, because that's not the problem.' Fox News's Bret Baier then said: 'Well, I'm going to ask a question to everyone here on the stage. Say you had a deal, a real spending cuts deal, ten to one, as — as Byron said, spending cuts to tax increases. Speaker [referring to Newt Gingrich], you're already shaking your head. But who on this stage would walk away from that deal? Can you raise your hand if you feel so strongly about not raising taxes, you'd walk away on the ten to one deal?' All the candidates (Rick Santorum, Herman Cain, Ron Paul, Michelle Bachman, Tim Pawlenty, Jim Huntsman, Newt Gingrich and notably Mitt Romney) raised their hands.

21 See Jonathan D. Ostry et al., 'Fiscal Space', IMF Staff Position Note, SPN/10/11 (Washington DC: International Monetary Fund, 1 September 2010).

22 J. Bradford DeLong and Lawrence H. Summers, 'Fiscal Policy in a Depressed Economy', 20 March 2012, http://www.brookings. edu/~/media/Files/Programs/ES/BPEA/2012_spring_bpea_papers/2012_spring_BPEA_delongsummers.pdf.

23 See Erik Jones, 'Merkel's Folly', *Survival*, vol. 52, no. 3, June–July 2010, pp. 21–38.

24 Erik Jones, 'Italy's Sovereign Debt Crisis', *Survival*, vol. 54, no. 1, February–March 2012, pp. 83–110.

25 Christine Lagarde, 'Global Risks Are Rising, But There Is a Path to Recovery: Remarks at Jackson Hole', Jackson Hole, Wyoming, 27 August 2011, http://www.imf.org/external/np/speeches/2011/082711.htm.

26 Martin Wolf, 'A Fragile Europe Must Change Fast', *Financial Times*, 23 May 2012, p. 13. On the case for eurobonds, see Jones, 'Merkel's Folly', p. 34.

27 The line of argument developed in this subsection builds on two essays by Erik Jones: 'Shifting the Focus: The New Political Economy of Global Macroeconomic Imbalances', *SAIS Review*, vol. 29, no. 2, Summer–Fall 2009, pp. 61–73; and 'Macroeconomic Imbalances and the Sovereign Debt Crisis', in Kurt Huebner (ed.), *Europe, Canada, and the Comprehensive Trade Agreement* (London: Routledge, 2011), pp. 289–305.

28 Riccardo Hausmann and Federico Sturzenegger, *Global Imbalances or Bad Account? The Missing Dark Matter in the Wealth of Nations*, CID Working Paper No. 124 (Cambridge,

MA: Center for International Development, Harvard University, January 2006 – revised September 2006).

29 Herbert Stein, Chairman of the Council of Economic Advisers under Presidents Nixon and Ford, articulated this eponymous principle: 'If something cannot go on forever, it will stop.'

30 Stephen M. Walt, 'The End of the American Era', *The National Interest*, November–December 2011, pp. 6–16.

31 See 'USA Debt Downgrade', Reuters, 6 August 2011, http://www.reuters.com/article/2011/08/06/us-usa-debt-downgrade-idUSTRE7746VF20110806.

32 Valery Giscard D'Estaigne, quoted in Pierre Olivier Gourinchas and Helene Rey, 'From World Banker to World Venture Capitalist: U.S. External Adjustment and the Exorbitant Privilege', in Richard H. Clarida (ed.), *G7 Current Account Imbalances: Sustainability and Adjustment* (Chicago, IL: National Bureau of Economic Research and University of Chicago Press, 2007), pp. 11–66, http://socrates.berkeley.edu/~pog/academic/gourinchas_rey_exorbitant.pdf.

33 Kennedy, *The Rise and Fall of Great Powers*.

34 David P. Calleo, *The Imperious Economy* (Cambridge, MA: Harvard University Press, 1982).

35 David P. Calleo, 'Obama's Dilemma: Enraged Opponents or Disappointed Followers', p. 7, http://bcjournal.org/wp-content/uploads/2010/05/calleo-from-bcjia-mag_final-2.pdf.

36 For a good overview of China's position from a variety of different perspectives, see Morris Goldstein and Nicholas R. Lardy (eds), *Debating China's Exchange Rate Policy* (Washington DC: Peterson Institute for International Economics, 2008).

37 See Joanne Gowa, *Closing the Gold Window: Domestic Politics and the End of Bretton Woods* (Ithaca, NY: Cornell University Press, 1983); Arnold Kling, *Unchecked and Unbalanced* (Lanham, MD: Rowman & Littlefield, 2010).

38 Robert Skidelsky, 'The Economic Crisis and the International Order', Plenary Speech, the IISS Global Strategic Review, 13 September 2009, Geneva, http://www.iiss.org/conferences/global-strategic-review/global-strategic-review-2009/plenary-sessions-and-speeches-2009/lord-robert-skidelsky/.

39 *Ibid.*

40 Wolf, *Fixing Global Finance*, pp. 58–59.

41 Skidelsky, 'The Economic Crisis and the International Order'.

42 Bill Emmott, 'The world economy is Osama's biggest victim', *The Times*, 5 September 2011, http://www.billemmott.com/article.php?id=333.

Chapter Five

1   For this and the following quotations, see 'Remarks by the President on the Defense Strategic Review', 5 January 2012, http://www.whitehouse.gov/the-press-office/2012/01/05/remarks-president-defense-strategic-review.

2   See 'Sustaining U.S. Global Leadership: Priorities for 21st Century Defense' (Washington DC: Department of Defense, January 2012); and, 'Defense Budget Priorities and Choices' (Washington DC: Department of Defense, January 2012).

3   See, for example, Baker Spring, 'Obama's Defense Budget Makes Protecting America Its Lowest Priority', Heritage Foundation Backgrounder no. 2658, 1 March 2012, http://www.heritage.org/research/reports/2012/03/obamas-defense-budget-makes-protecting-america-its-lowest-priority.

4   *The Military Balance 2012* (London: Routledge for the IISS, 2012), p. 44.

5   'Fiscal Year Budget Request 2013: Overview', (Washington DC: Comptroller, Department of Defense, February 2012) pp. 1–2.

6   *The Military Balance 2012*, p. 45.

7   *Ibid.*, p. 32.

8   Fred Kaplan, 'Paul Ryan's Risky Ideas', *Slate Magazine*, 5 April 2012, http://www.slate.com/articles/news_and_politics/war_stories/2012/04/budget_chairman_paul_ryan_would_let_the_military_make_its_own_budget_.html.

9   See Office of Management and Budget, 'Outlays by Superfunction and Function 1940–2017' (Washington DC: US Government Printing Office, 2010), http://www.whitehouse.gov/sites/default/files/omb/budget/fy2013/assets/hist03z1.xls.

10 This is not a new argument in the field of international political economy. Charles Kindleberger sketched the requirements for hegemonic stability in his 1975 study of the Great Depression. See Charles P. Kindleberger, *The World in Depression, 1929–1939* (Berkeley, CA: University of California Press, 1975). Specifically, Kindleberger argued that a successful hegemon must have the abilities to underwrite the system by acting as an open market for distressed goods, to enforce the rules impartially, to provide moral leadership, and to act as a lender of last resort. Over time, like-minded scholars have emphasised the importance of psychological factors as well. See, for example, George A. Akerlof and Robert J. Schiller, *Animal Spirits: How Human Psychology Drives the Economy, and Why It Matters for Global Capitalism* (Princeton, NJ: Princeton University Press, 2009).

11 The late 1960s and early 1970s witnessed an important flourishing in the study of power. Classical

realists like E.H. Carr or Hans J. Morgenthau had focused on the exercise of power as a function of wealth and capabilities. See E.H. Carr, *The Twenty Years Crisis, 1919–1939* (London: PaperMac, Second Edition, 1995 [1946]), pp. 97–134; Hans J. Morgenthau, *Politics Among Nations: The Struggle for Power and Peace* (New York: Alfred A. Knopf, Second Edition, 1958 [1954]), pp. 93–152. But the writers of the late 1960s and early 1970s were more concerned with the possibility that groups without obvious endowments could nevertheless force changes to the status quo. Traditional concepts of power were set aside in favour of new relational notions that underscored the importance of managing interdependence, manipulating uncertainty and redefining the possible in a changed world.

12 Kagan, *The Return of History and the End of Dreams*; Fareed Zakaria, *The Post-American World* (New York: W.W. Norton & Company, 2008); Dominic Wilson and Roopa Purushothaman, 'Dreaming with BRICs: The Path to 2050', *Global Economics Paper, No. 99* (New York: Goldman Sachs, 1 October 2003); Goldman Sachs Economics Group, *BRICs and Beyond* (New York: Goldman Sachs, 2007), http://www.goldmansachs.com/our-thinking/brics/BRICs-and-Beyond.html.

13 Friedman, *The World Is Flat*; Zakaria, *The Post-American World*.

14 Jagdish Bhagwati, *Termites in the Trading System: How Preferential Trading Agreements Undermine Free Trade* (New York: Oxford University Press, 2008).

15 Richard N. Cooper, *The Economics of Interdependence: Economic Policy in the Atlantic Community* (New York: McGraw-Hill for the Council on Foreign Relations, 1968) pp. 260–4. Cooperation is never easy, but it is more effective than trying to go it alone and it is more durable than trying to compel others. This is the central insight in Hannah Arendt's work *On Violence*. Arendt uses the notion of violence to distinguish between power and coercion. Her basic point is that power lies in collective action: 'The extreme form of power is All against One, the extreme form of violence is One against All.' What she reveals with this distinction is the importance of legitimacy and acceptance – not for any given actor or groups of actors, but for the underlying rules of the game. Actors do not possess power by dint of their resources, rather they are 'empowered by a certain number of people to act in their name'. Once this group withdraws its support, the power itself withers away. See Hannah Arendt, *On Violence* (New York: Harcourt Brace Jovanovich, 1969), pp. 42–4.

16 Mancur Olson, *The Logic of Collective Action: Public Goods and the Theory of Groups* (Cambridge, MA: Harvard University Press, 1971).

17 Spencer Ackerman, 'America's Global Outlook, at an Inflection Point', *Washington Independent*, 28 May 2010, http://washingtoninde-pendent.com/85916/americas-global-outlook-at-an-inflection-point. Many thanks to John Gans for bringing this to my attention.

18 *The National Security Strategy of the United States of America* (Washington DC: The White House, May 2010), p. 2.

19 *Ibid.*, p. 41.

20 Erik Jones, 'Shifting the Focus: The New Political Economy of Global Macroeconomic Imbalances', *SAIS Review*, vol. 29, no. 2, Summer–Fall 2009, pp. 61–73.

21 See, for example, Lester Thurow, *The Zero-Sum Society: Distribution and the Possibilities for Economic Change* (New York: Penguin, 1981 [1980]); and Mancur Olson, *The Rise and Decline of Nations: Economic Growth, Stagflation, and Social Rigidities* (New Haven, CT: Yale University Press, 1982).

22 This is a recurring theme in the writings of *Financial Times* columnist Martin Wolf. See Martin Wolf, *Fixing Global Finance* (New Haven, CT: Yale University Press, 2009).

23 This data is taken from the United Nations and is available upon request.

24 Recent scholarship suggests this has always been the case, even during the period between the two World Wars. See Bear F. Braumoeller, 'The Myth of American Isolationism', *Foreign Policy Analysis*, vol. 6, no. 4, October 2010, pp. 349–71.

25 The transcript of these debates is available online at http://www.debates.org/pages/trans2004a_p.html.

26 From a speech by former Defense Secretary Robert Gates, Brussels, 10 June 2011, available at http://blogs.wsj.com/washwire/2011/06/10/transcript-of-defense-secretary-gatess-speech-on-natos-future/.

Conclusion

1   Henry Kissinger, *On China* (London: Penguin Books, 2012), p. 425.

2   Paul Krugman, 'Europe's Economic Suicide', *New York Times*, 15 April 2012, http://www.nytimes.com/2012/04/16/opinion/krugman-europes-economic-suicide.html.

3   James Dobbins, 'Coping with a Nuclearizing Iran', *Survival*, vol. 53, no. 6 (December 2011–January 2012) p. 46.

4   Obama affirmed his declaration that containment of a nuclear Iran was not an option. During his speech to the America Israel Public Affairs Committee's annual policy conference, in Washington DC, on 4 March 2012, he said: 'I made a commitment to the American people and said that we would use all elements of American power to pressure Iran and prevent it from acquiring a nuclear weapon. And that is what we have done.' See http://www.politico.com/news/stories/0312/73588.html.

5   Allin and Simon, *The Sixth Crisis*, pp. 158–60.

6   Adam Ward, personal communication with authors, May 2012; we are indebted to Adam for much of this line of thinking regarding China.

7   Leon Panetta, speech to the IISS Shangri-La Dialogue, 2 June 2012, http://www.iiss.org/conferences/the-shangri-la-dialogue/shangri-la-dialogue-2012/speeches/first-plenary-session/leon-panetta/.

8   James Dobbins, again, is astute on this subject. He writes: 'It is certainly true that China could become the most powerful adversary the United States has ever faced. Over the next 20 years, China's gross domestic product (GDP) and defence budget could exceed those of the United States. If it chose, China could therefore become a more capable opponent than either the Soviet Union or Nazi Germany at their peak, neither of which ever approached America's economic might ...[However, it] is important to begin any such analysis by recognising that China is seeking neither territorial aggrandisement nor ideological sway over its neighbours. It shows no interest in matching US military expenditures, achieving a comparable global reach, or assuming defence commitments beyond its immediate periphery. Such intentions might change, but if so, the United States would probably receive considerable warning, given the lead times needed to develop such capabilities.' See Dobbins, 'War with China', forthcoming in *Survival*, vol. 54, no. 4 (August–September 2012).

Adelphi books are published eight times a year by Routledge Journals, an imprint of Taylor & Francis, 4 Park Square, Milton Park, Abingdon, Oxfordshire OX14 4RN, UK.

A subscription to the institution print edition, ISSN 1944-5571, includes free access for any number of concurrent users across a local area network to the online edition, ISSN 1944-558X. Taylor & Francis has a flexible approach to subscriptions enabling us to match individual libraries' requirements. This journal is available via a traditional institutional subscription (either print with free online access, or online-only at a discount) or as part of the Strategic, Defence and Security Studies subject package or Strategic, Defence and Security Studies full text package. For more information on our sales packages please visit www.tandfonline.com/librarians_pricinginfo_journals.

2012 Annual Adelphi Subscription Rates			
Institution	£525	$924 USD	€777
Individual	£239	$407 USD	€324
Online only	£473	$832 USD	€699

Dollar rates apply to subscribers outside Europe. Euro rates apply to all subscribers in Europe except the UK and the Republic of Ireland where the pound sterling price applies. All subscriptions are payable in advance and all rates include postage. Journals are sent by air to the USA, Canada, Mexico, India, Japan and Australasia. Subscriptions are entered on an annual basis, i.e. January to December. Payment may be made by sterling cheque, dollar cheque, international money order, National Giro, or credit card (Amex, Visa, Mastercard).

For a complete and up-to-date guide to Taylor & Francis journals and books publishing programmes, and details of advertising in our journals, visit our website: **http://www.tandfonline.com.**

Ordering information:
USA/Canada: Taylor & Francis Inc., Journals Department, 325 Chestnut Street, 8th Floor, Philadelphia, PA 19106, USA. **UK/Europe/Rest of World:** Routledge Journals, T&F Customer Services, T&F Informa UK Ltd., Sheepen Place, Colchester, Essex, CO3 3LP, UK.

Advertising enquiries to:
USA/Canada: The Advertising Manager, Taylor & Francis Inc., 325 Chestnut Street, 8th Floor, Philadelphia, PA 19106, USA. Tel: +1 (800) 354 1420. Fax: +1 (215) 625 2940. **UK/Europe/Rest of World**: The Advertising Manager, Routledge Journals, Taylor & Francis, 4 Park Square, Milton Park, Abingdon, Oxfordshire OX14 4RN, UK. Tel: +44 (0) 20 7017 6000. Fax: +44 (0) 20 7017 6336.

The print edition of this journal is printed on ANSI conforming acid-free paper by Bell & Bain, Glasgow, UK.